ON THE
ANVIL

On The Anvil

The art of learning leadership from experience

ROBERT WARREN

HIGHLAND BOOKS

ISBN 0 946616 66 3

Cover design by Diane Drummond

Photograph: Roger Maytum

Printed in Great Britain for
HIGHLAND BOOKS
Broadway House, The Broadway,
Crowborough, East Sussex TN6 1HQ
by Richard Clay Ltd, Bungay, Suffolk
Typeset by Rowland Phototypesetting Ltd,
Bury St Edmunds, Suffolk

CONTENTS

Introduction   7

PART ONE: The art of learning from experience

Chapter One . . . . The anvil of experience   15
Chapter Two . . . . The point of learning   27
Chapter Three . . . . A framework for learning   40
Chapter Four . . . . Discovering God's agenda   54

PART TWO: Practising the art

Chapter Five . . . . Discovering vision   69
Chapter Six . . . . Transferring vision   84
Chapter Seven . . . . Implementing change   103
Chapter Eight . . . . Taking people with you   117
Chapter Nine . . . . Solving problems   131
Chapter Ten . . . . Structuring for growth   145
Chapter Eleven . . . . Managing to survive   162
Chapter Twelve . . . . Keeping going   176

INTRODUCTION

Several causes have prompted me to add to the literature on church leadership.

First, I have wanted to tell the 'story behind the story' of the growth of St Thomas's church. My first book, *In the Crucible*, tells of the growth of the church from one hundred and fifty to over one thousand worshippers a Sunday. Growth does not happen without effective leadership. This book therefore both completes the story and complements it with some explanation of how leadership was exercised. However, it is written on the assumption that the reader has not read my first book – though it obviously gives a fuller background to what I say here.

Second, has been the desire to develop an aspect of leadership that receives scant coverage in the many otherwise excellent books on leadership that I have read, namely how we can learn from experience. I am well aware of the considerable library of books, both secular and Christian, on leadership. However, they are predominantly theory: good theory, I hasten to add. Theory, I am also sure, that was learned the hard way – from experience. But *how* such lessons were learned is rarely touched on. Yet the process of learning the skills of church leadership that I have been through over the years has convinced me that *experience* is the key to effective learning in the area of leadership. Or, rather, it is not just experience, but the constant process of reflecting on experience – both good and bad – which has been at the heart of my learning.

The incarnation teaches us that God's highest form of

revelation is not at the purely rational or theoretical level, but in a person: in the life, work, and death of his Son Jesus Christ. Christian truth is truth incarnate, and it should therefore come as no surprise that Christian learning is modelled on the incarnation. For this reason I have wanted to go beyond simply telling the story of lessons learned, and to reflect on how those lessons have been learned. This has been new and uncharted territory for me and I have found it a fascinating and stretching experience to explore some of the issues involved.

Third, in the process of thinking about my own experience, a framework for learning has emerged which has greatly helped me to understand my own experience of leadership. I am glad of the opportunity to share it with a wider audience through this book. I hope that others will find it as illuminating as I have done.

The result of this process of reflection on my experience is a book in two distinct parts. In the first four chapters I look at the subject of learning from experience and seek to develop a framework in which to understand and handle such learning. In the second part of the book I then go on to explore the practice of learning from experience. This second part is itself in two sections. In the first I look at the discovery, development and implementing of vision, since vision is the basic ingredient of leadership. In the other section I consider the material we actually have to handle, namely the church or group as it is with all its problems and limitations, and ourselves. This second part of the book is basically an attempt to show how the more theoretical first part can work in practice.

However, before going any further I want at the outset to issue a health warning about reading such a book as this! Inevitably it contains details of specific things we have done, and programmes we have developed. I am concerned that the reader does not attempt to read the book simply in order to copy our practices.

An illustration, which I first heard John Wimber use, expresses well what I am seeking to say. John likened church leadership to the construction of a building. First you need to dig deep in order to lay the foundations. This relates to the *values* on which the whole church will be built. Then comes the superstructure which represents the *principles*. Next, the internal walls are built; these represent the *policies* on which the church will operate. Finally,

8

furnishings are placed in each room. The furniture represents the *practices* or *programmes* that have been developed.

The important thing to notice is that each stage emerges out of a previous one with the end result that the practices should express the values. However, it is the practices we see most clearly, while the values remain hidden from view. All too often, leaders latch onto the programme or structure or way of doing things and copy them without any thought of the underlying values. Such copying rarely has the desired effect. The health warning, therefore, is to beware of thinking that copying a particular programme will of itself produce the same result as it did in the original setting.

An example will make the point. During my time at St Thomas's, we scrapped two morning services in order to combine them in one, and later scrapped that one service so as to form two morning services from it. Neither programme is right of itself, but only if it best expresses the values which we hold. When we joined everyone together it was out of a conviction (value) that being together as one church was what mattered most. When, seventeen years later, we reversed that decision it was in order to express better the need to make space for the newcomer within our fellowship. Other ways had been found of expressing our unity, now our mission was the primary motivation (value).

'Are two morning services better than one?' is therefore a nonsense question. It is like asking whether a car is better than an aeroplane. Neither question can be answered unless we know what sort of journey we are wanting to make. I labour the point because it is one of the most common mistakes in leadership – the adopting of the programme of another church without consideration of the issues lying behind that programme or its setting.

Having said this, I hope there will be many practical ideas which the reader can pick up from what follows, but I urge a careful reflection on the purpose and aim as the only way to assess whether a particular change of practice is actually likely to be beneficial.

I want to say a word about those to whom this book is addressed. The principles are applied in the first place to the full-time leader of the local church. However, practically all that I say is equally relevant to anyone seeking to exercise leadership in a Christian work. My hope is that a home group leader, a youth leader, or the leader of any team of Christians working together, will find here help both to understand and to develop the leadership to which they have been called. Although I write now as the vicar of a church with over one thousand worshippers, the principles which I seek to establish are applicable to any church or group of any size or at any stage. Indeed, in a recent conversation with a Christian businessman I was fascinated to discover that the framework for learning which I have developed exactly fitted his experience of seeking to function Christianly in the business world.

Naturally, I have earthed these lessons primarily in my experience of leadership at St Thomas's church. However, my desire is not to 'sell' our own particular solutions, but rather to stimulate the readers, with their own unique personalities and church situations, to develop the skill of learning church leadership by reflecting on the experiences they have had. My prayer is that this story of discovery and struggle, joy and heartache, will encourage others to press on in the noble *servant* role of leadership for the spread of the gospel and in the work of the kingdom.

Finally, some words of thanks. So many have been examples to me that I could not name them all, but I do want to express my appreciation to some who have had a particular contribution to the writing of this book. Richard Laughlin, a wise friend and counsellor, and former churchwarden, and himself an author, has been of great help in reading and commenting on the series of drafts this book has gone through. He has been a skilful and affirming tutor to me. Derek Frank, a colleague on the staff team over the past two years, has helped me to grasp the distinction between considering what lessons we have been learning and *how* those lessons have been learned. His sharp analytical mind has dug deep into my experience and enabled me to get in touch with the underlying patterns of my much more intuitive way of working. His help has itself been a learning process for me.

My wholehearted thanks go to my wife Ann, who has been a constant support in the often painful learning process recounted in this book. She has borne much of the heat of the battle – or rather – of the anvil! This book could obviously never have been written if there had not been a congregation of people willing to face constant upheaval and growth, and who continually surprise me with their maturity, patience and courageous obedience to God.

It is to him that the thanksgiving of all who have been in any way involved in this story and book is due above all. He it is who has proved both present, faithful and persistent in taking us all onto the anvil of experience and shaping us more to his purposes. May he be honoured and his church helped by what follows.

PART ONE

*The art of learning
from experience*

Chapter One

THE ANVIL OF EXPERIENCE

Even before writing of the growth of St Thomas's, Crookes, in Sheffield (in *In the Crucible*) I had frequently been asked the embarrassing question: 'To what do you attribute the success of your church?' I hastened first to point out that, although I knew what the questioner meant, one of the causes of the growth is that neither I nor the church see it as 'my' church. It belongs to God and is his creation. The growth is the consequence of our seeking continually to discover what he wants to do with his church. I usually next point out that if the questioner were a member of the church they would be unlikely to call it successful. Again, paradoxically the growth is not unrelated to a healthy slice of honesty about what it is really like. We may have one thousand in church on a Sunday, but that still leaves seven thousand parishioners untouched by us or any other church. Moreover, there are so many points at which we realise that we are searching for answers, that 'successful' just does not fit the feel of the church.

Yet clearly a work of God is taking place, and we have found significant answers to a number of questions. But this actually adds to my difficulty in answering this question, especially as it is often asked by church leaders longing to see substantial growth released in their situation. Such people come eager to glean any insights that might help them in their ministry (just as I do when visiting other churches).

My dilemma is this. The most crucial insight I have learned over the years is something that canno be passed on directly. It is that leadership has been developed on the anvil of experience, which is a totally non-transferable commodity! My experience, like the experience of everyone else, is unique. So what I can do – and will attempt to do in this book – is to help others to use the key resource that every person has in abundance: experience. It is that, I am convinced, that God intends to use to shape leaders and churches into the people and communities he desires them to be. It is a painful method, but there is good news wrapped up in it. Experience is one thing we all have. There is hope for everyone. We may not have had any formal training, or it may have been a long time ago, or of limited relevance, but we all have experience. The vital lesson to learn, therefore, is how to harness it for personal and church growth.

The unique role of experience was drawn to my attention even before leaving theological college. In the final week we heard lectures by some of the most experienced leaders of youth work. Yet, after over ten hours of copious note-taking, I really knew no more than before. It was the lack of experience which prevented me from learning. Six months later I was embroiled in youth work, struggling to cope with the youth culture of Manchester and a group of exuberant young Christians keen to evangelise the newly emerging drug scene. Just half an hour with any of those men would have transformed my work. Before, I had not retained the answers because I had not even grasped the problems. Experience taught me the problems – at speed. Then I was wide open to receiving answers!

Life can be a great educator; but whether it turns out to be so depends on a number of factors. Information and instruction give us the tools for learning, but without experience little may result. Not that experience is enough by itself, nor does it always ensure that we learn the right things. All of us know people who say that life has taught them never to trust people – or God. It is experience which is the anvil on which we are shaped as people and as leaders. Our personalities, our thinking and choosing, together with the resulting actions, constitute the metal on which the hammer falls.

When called into leadership in a work of God, we need to undergo divine shaping and reshaping until we are forged into the instrument that he can use. Uncomfortable though it often is, this process is in the loving and wise hands of the divine Blacksmith. He alone is able to bring out the best in us; and he alone knows our breaking point too. Yet it is for us to choose and to keep choosing to put ourselves on that anvil, for his shaping. If there is one key insight I have to share about learning leadership it is the willingness to keep choosing this availability to God and to personal growth even when there is much within us which longs for an easier way. We will always be people in the making, so this is a lifetime's calling and a continual choice.

Precious Metal

I came to be on God's anvil quite unwittingly at first. Like everyone else I have a natural protectiveness towards the things I value most in life – especially myself and my own identity. Yet love calls us beyond that instinct for preservation into the realm of risk in self-giving. This is supremely so in our encounter with the love of God. His love calls out of us the response of self-offering. For me, this has proved to be a slowly dawning realisation of who I am, and what I was therefore bringing to God as the metal of my being for his shaping.

The starting point in the process was the sense of calling I had received to the ordained ministry while still a teenager. It happened at the boys' camp at which I came to faith, though a couple of years later. I had the privilege of having Michael Green as my dormitory officer. I was talking with conviction about the state of the church and what it ought to do, with all the confidence and lack of knowledge you would expect from a newly converted teenager. Michael listened patiently and then said, 'If you feel like that, you should be ordained.' I was shaken and embarrassed, and immediately suggested that we had a game of squash. Although I managed to change the subject quickly with Michael Green, I had no such luck with God. That phrase 'you ought to be ordained' kept ringing in my ears. Back at school, six weeks later, it was still there and stronger. I realised that I had to do something about it.

I wrote to my parents. They had previously made it quite clear that my earlier hopes of being an airline pilot did not meet with their approval. Although they had come to faith at the same time as I had, I sensed that ordination would not meet with approval.

In fact they were delighted. Their seeming coolness was motivated by a desire not to put any pressure on, or even express their preference for me, but rather to allow God to lead if that was his way. Despite pressures and temptations to quit, it is this call that has stayed with me over the years and has been the foundation of my ministry.

Allied (and alloyed?) to the call God has given me are convictions about God and life. One of the most important was, and still is, that scripture is God's word to man: a supernatural conduit of truth that touches man – most often where it is hurting. During my time at Cambridge University this conviction was tested – sometimes close to destruction. It was hard, but enormously valuable work, integrating an academic approach to a book that had begun life, for me, as the oracles of God. There were moments when, in attitude at least, I had to stand before my tutors saying 'I have no answer to your rational explanations of the texts of scripture, but I have encountered God through them.' For the Christian, the scriptures are a vital instrument in God's hands to shape the heated metal of our personalities into his design – conforming each of us to the image of Christ.

A third element of the metal to be placed on God's anvil is what I brought to God as a person. I once heard it said that a mature person is someone with a true understanding of their strengths and weaknesses. In the early years of ministry, and marriage, I found that a hard task. The difficulty was continually brought home to me by the series of fine visiting preachers who came to Holy Trinity, Platt, Manchester at the invitation of Michael Baughen the vicar, while I was curate there. I was inspired by them, and for some while sought to pattern my life, ministry, and personality on them. But within weeks the vision had faded and I knew that I was not that sort of person, by which time another had come and the whole process had been repeated.

Since those days, and with the passing years, I have found a growing awareness of – and confidence in – who I am. Not that this has been an entirely happy discovery. One of the more disturbing findings has been that I, and I suspect others too, have no strength that cannot at the same time become a weakness. A sense of humour can mask a fear of confronting conflict. An ability to organise can be a way of hiding from people. An openness to others and their ideas can result in being taken in and fooled by the manipulative person. The ability to weigh things carefully can stop us taking swift and decisive action when occasion demands it.

Yet, as I stood on the threshold of ordination, although I was aware of some of these things, I was about to discover that there was much in the alloy of my being which had yet to come onto the anvil. Even within one week of this great event, for which I had been preparing for eight years, I had little idea of what even the next few days were to hold.

The timing should have alerted me to the unpredictability of the ways of God, and to the strange mixture of joy and pain, hope and fear that lay ahead. I was due to be ordained at Michaelmas (late September) but five days before ordination I went down with stomach pains and was rushed into hospital with acute appendicitis. I ended that week having hands laid on me lower down than expected! Not that the three-month delay was wasted. It was put to good use through my engagement to Ann. So, three months late, I entered the ministry in different shape – with a fiancée, but without an appendix! It was a picture of the joy and unpredictability of being in God's hands for him to shape in such a way that I was fit to minister.

Hammer Blows

Not only was I unaware of the action-packed path that was to lead up to ordination, but I was also almost totally ignorant of the fact that the coals had been heated and the hammer was about to be skilfully played not just on my ministry, but on me as a person. It took some while, as I threw myself into the ministry, to notice that God had become my blacksmith and was turning his attention to me and my convictions. Since then my greatest problem with God has been that he loves me more than I do. I can cope with my faults, failures, and unbelief. I do not like them, but I can be merciful to them and give them house-room. To do anything else would disturb *me*! Yet God's love is such that he will not give such things house-room. However closely attached to them we are, he prizes us apart from them: often in the refiner's fire. One of the first areas in which I experienced those refining fires was in my understanding of my calling.

I was going to be a clergyman – if, as subsequently happened, that call was confirmed by the wider church. But what was the task of a clergyman? Later experience uncovered what my real expectations had been. My unconscious assumption was that I would be majoring on preaching and giving Bible readings. By the end of my first curacy I had come to realise that the ministry is primarily about *people*. The gospel is about helping people to know God and to live in an awareness of him.

Learning to relate to ordinary people in a parish very close to inner-city Manchester was a crash course in humanity. Realising that the job was to help such people to faith, and on in the faith, came as something of a shock. I had not realised that this was what the ministry was all about. However I was in, and it was clear that God does not go back on his decisions or calling. *He* knew what the ministry was all about. There was no need for me to opt out. Rather I needed to opt into relating to people in the way he had intended by giving me that call.

As I have reflected on the baptism of Jesus (his ordination), I have become convinced that one of the important strands in the meaning of that event was preparation for self-giving service. Such self-giving can only take place out of a secure personality. Ministry so easily slips into meeting the needs of the minister (the need to be needed, or the need to achieve) rather than the needs of those to whom he is sent. The Father's words were affirming: 'You are my son, whom I love; with you I am well pleased' (Lk 3.22). We can enter the world of another only when we are secure enough as people to be self-forgetful.

Further major reshaping of my understanding about the ministry came a couple of years later, at St James's, Fordhouses, Wolverhampton. Handling a church on my own for the first time, I discovered that effective ministry involves the ability to *lead people*. I had watched Michael Baughen take a group of people and build them into a church family. A group identity, confidence, and sense of purpose had grown steadily.

I began to realise at Fordhouses that there is far more to the ministry than one-to-one relationships with each member of the church (important though these relationships are). The church is

20

not just a collection of individuals. It is a community. I was in at the deep end, discovering that my job was to draw a group of people together, help them to establish a clear identity, nurture their faith and foster their service of God. The creation of such a community or group identity is no easy task in the individualistic society in which we live; but it is the first and crucial stage in the process of leading others. I was fortunate to be handling such a small group that everyone knew everyone. Nonetheless much fundamental reshaping of my thinking still had to take place through the hammer blows of that experience.

One of the losses to the church through the demise of the Authorised Version of the Bible is that our translations make no distinction in English between the singular 'thou' and plural 'you'. Watch yourself, and most preachers, and you will find that we always assume a personal interpretation of all commands and promises. Yet most of them are addressed to communities and spoken of communities. For example, 'You are the light of the world' is likely to be read as speaking of such things as personal morality in our work situations. When we see it as primarily addressed to a team of disciples it takes on a much richer perspective. 'You, in the way you relate together, and order your community life, are a demonstration to the world of the Trinity – distinct Persons working together in the context of love.' Obviously that does not deny the personal level; but it does take us well beyond it.

It is one of the joys and wonders of the ministry that we are called to co-operate with God in *creating a community* that is effective for him in the world. The more creativity there is in work the more job-satisfaction we are likely to experience. Moreover, the ministry is working in one of the most complex mediums that any artist can work with – people. Additionally, the Christian is involved with the whole spiritual and super-natural dimension of life. It is good to realise both the privilege and the demands of all Christian leadership when we see it in the context of creating community out of a body of people, even if – like King David – our material looks a little unpromising. Many ministers, and leaders in Christian endeavours, will identify with David's task:

> David left Gath and escaped to the cave of Adullam. When his brothers and his father's household heard about it, they went down to him there. All those who were in distress or in debt or discontented gathered around him, and he became their leader. About four hundred men were with him.
>
> (I Sam 22.1, 2)

To bring into existence, or to mature and develop, a believing community is one of the most demanding and exciting tasks. It was one of the first tasks that Jesus took on in calling the twelve disciples and building them into a cohesive group. It was a costly calling for Jesus and, as I was to discover, for me too. The reshaping of my understanding of ministry, which began in those early days, has continued into the present. Constant new challenges to my ability to lead people have generated fresh hammer blows of experience. Now I know that learning can come out of every experience. Harnessing the ability to learn did not, however, come immediately or without cost.

Personal Meltdown
By the time I arrived in Sheffield, I had realised that this learning and reshaping process was to be a way of life and not some brief post-ordination training for the especially inexperienced. Nevertheless, I was far from realising how personal this training by experience could become.

Within eighteen months of arriving to lead the growing church of St Thomas's, I found myself facing a multi-dimensional darkness. Preaching and pastoral work seemed to lack any life-giving vitality and I was struggling for a sense of direction. The calling to the ordained ministry with which I began had somehow become lost on the way, or overlaid by activity, or simply broken in the battle.

God's way through did not appeal to my sense of humour – at the time. The heat was turned up sufficiently to allow a profound reshaping of my experience of him. I was no enthusiast for speaking in tongues but found it to be the light at the end of a long, dark spiritual tunnel. I was not, and am not, a person who shows my emotions easily, and yet I experienced a three-week period of almost unremitting tears. Through a renewing experience of the Holy Spirit (which I have told more fully in *In the*

Crucible) I realised that nothing I was or held dear was sacrosanct from divine attention. My self-understanding, my convictions about the scriptures and the place of experience in Christian living, and the underlying motivation for ministry all came under close scrutiny. The fire of God's holiness, fanned by the bellows (or wind) of God's Spirit on the anvil of experience, made what I had previously thought of as the solid metal of my personality turn to something much more like potter's clay. It certainly felt as if God was 'going hammer and tongs' at me.

Two things stand out from that anvil experience. First is the new intimacy with God which was established. It is not a fixed state but a relationship that blows both hot and cold, yet it has remained on a level significantly above where I had been before.

Second was the transformation in my ministry from achieving to receiving. I discovered that Christian service is all about *God's* plans, and *God's* grace to fulfil them, not about my plans to achieve things for God. Before, the focus had been on achieving things for God. After my encounter with the Holy Spirit my perspective changed. I saw God as much more evidently the one calling the tune and pulling the strings. I saw him, in a new way, as the initiator of the church's life – and the writer of its agenda. I was moving from plans-to-serve-him to waiting-for-orders. It was a risky step. I could no longer plot the course ahead, because the next step was not in my control, it was in God's hands. The agenda of the church was God's gift. Our task shifted from planning to listening; from achieving to receiving. Not, I hasten to add, that we stopped planning and organisation: if anything they increased. But they played a different role. They were no longer the (man-made) means of bringing in the harvest: they were simply the tools necessary to contain the harvest that God was giving. This was a profound shift in my perception of leadership.

Towards a Thesis Statement
By this time, after ten years in the ordained ministry, I was beginning to understand something of the process that the Blacksmith was employing. It was well expressed by two con-secutive prayers prayed at one of our monthly central prayer meetings. Someone had prayed 'Lord, we thank you that you

accept us just as we are.' Quick as a flash, John Foote (a retired doctor who had been ordained, and joined the staff at the end of the 70s) prayed 'And thank you, Lord, that you do not leave us as we are!'

I had brought myself and my training, understanding, and my experience to the anvil. Rather than being content with the gift as it was, I found that God was committed to reshaping me for his own purposes. Only as I allowed him to put all that I held most dear (from biblical doctrines to personal habits and attitudes) into the fire of his love, and then – on the secure bedrock of his word – to hammer out, through experience, the mis-shapen and ill-formed quirks of me and my understanding, could living and developing ministry be exercised.

The heart of my learning about leadership in Christian work is that God is working on us before working on those to whom he sends us. We are called first to allow God actually to 'have' us, then to work on us, and – as a result of those two stages – to work through us. The 'ministry' which we call 'ours' is nothing other than the fruit of his 'ministry' to us. The reshaping of others into the image of Christ can only happen through us in as far as we have been, and continue to be, reshaped by God ourselves.

An essential to God 'having' us is our willingness to learn, and to be changed by that learning. The good news is that it is never too late to start learning from experience. However long ago we were in training, and whether or not we ever received any formal training, every day presents us with new opportunities for learning. Each day provides us with scope for reflection under God's leading on what has happened: what has gone well and what has not. We can begin today in this school of life.

The bad news is that it will cost us all we hold dear; for none of us will ever become more than a disciple or learner. Although none of us would ever say that we 'know it all' there are some tell-tale evidences when that is our unconscious assumption. The leader who reads little is acting on the belief that there is little to learn. The person who is defensive about criticism has put up a barrier against one of God's creative channels of learning. The leader who fails to analyse what is going on (and what is not going on) has largely closed the door on learning. The person whose attitude of false faith refuses to face the reality of failure shows resistance to learning.

It requires a long-term commitment to stay in the place of willingness to learn through the process of reflection on experience under the guidance of God. Much 'humble pie' has to be eaten on this journey. Yet this is the fare for effective Christian leaders.

Experience as a Sacrament

For those who desire to make that commitment to the journey of learning from experience, I share some words from Jean-Pierre de Caussade's spiritual classic *Self-Abandonment to Divine Providence*. In a moving passage he speaks about experience as the 'blessed sacrament of the present moment'. It is a great passage on which to meditate and to allow to enter our soul at the core of our personality – in order to prepare us for the art of learning 'on the anvil'; not just from the major hammer blows of life but from all the minor taps and knocks.

> There are few extraordinary features in the external life of the Blessed Virgin. At least Holy Scripture does not record any. Her life is represented as externally very simple and ordinary. She does and experiences the same things as other people in her state of life. She goes to visit her cousin Elizabeth, as her other relatives do. She takes shelter in a stable: a natural consequence of her poverty. She returns to Nazareth after having fled from the persecution of Herod. Jesus and Joseph live there with her, supporting themselves by the work of their hands. This provides their daily bread, but what is the divine food with which this material bread feeds the faith of Mary and Joseph? What is the sacrament of each of their sacred moments: What treasures of grace are contained in each of these moments underneath the commonplace appearances of the events that fill them? Outwardly these events are no different from those which happen to everyone, but the interior invisible element discerned by faith is nothing less than God himself performing great works. O bread of angels, heavenly manna, the pearl of the Gospels, *the sacrament of the present moment!* You present God in such lowly forms as the manger, the hay and straw! But to whom do you give him? 'You fill the hungry with good things.' God reveals himself to the humble in the humblest things, while the great who

never penetrate beneath the surface do not discover him even in great events.

Experience becomes a crucial factor in learning leadership, because the learning process that matters to God changes, by growth and stretching, the whole person – in order that truth may be incarnate. It includes the mind but does not primarily reside there. Learning is the constant process of reshaping the person and his or her perspectives to conform to the image of God and the likeness of Christ. It is a high and costly calling – and worth all that we have and are.

Not all of our experiences, particularly in the realm of Christian leadership, will be perceived as good. Yet there is nothing that, through God's grace, cannot be increasingly conformed to the image of God. Studying theories of leadership, vital as they are, will never achieve this by itself. There is no substitute for putting ourselves onto God's anvil, because Christian truth has to be truth incarnate. It has to permeate the whole of who and what we are. The basic question, before any other aspect of leadership can be faced, is whether we have made the choice to learn humbly in the context of God's love and care for us, from the multitude of experiences which he takes us through. Daily staying with this process, allowing the whole of what we are to go on the anvil, is the only true foundation for effective learning in the school of Christian leadership.

Chapter Two

THE POINT OF LEARNING

With a faculty of around two hundred students most economics lecturers at Cambridge had difficulty drawing one hundred of them to their lectures – all except for one man. He was a visiting American who had been in the Kennedy administration and was a fascinating speaker. I was studying economics for my first year before spending the next two on theology (a strange and stimulating mixture that was possible at Cambridge), and like others in the department, I invited friends studying quite unrelated subjects to hear this entertaining and informative man.

At the start of one of his lectures he began by asking for a show of hands of those who knew in which section of the American constitution such things as the powers of the President were outlined. For each specific question he gained just a few hands out of the four hundred who were packed into the lecture theatre on seats, steps, desk tops and the floor. After a dozen or so questions he gave up in frustration and said, 'You lot are really stupid.' Then he proceeded with yet another stimulating lecture.

The following week he began with an apology. 'You lot are not stupid, like I accused you of being last week,' he said, and went on to explain the differences, as he saw it, between American and English education. 'Our students,' he said 'have their heads crammed full with facts but they don't know how to use them: that is what I call stupid. You people know very few facts – but, boy, can you use them! You are not stupid, you are ignorant!'

I still do not know how valid the distinction between the two education systems was, but I do know that two distinctive

27

approaches to learning exist: gaining as much information as possible, or learning to think for yourself. How we progress in the realm of Christian leadership will largely depend on which approach we primarily adopt, and this choice hinges on what we consider to be the 'point of learning'.

Purpose

Entitling this chapter 'The point of learning' I have deliberately expressed a double meaning, through which to consider both where and why we learn. First, what is the *purpose* of our learning? The biblical perception is that learning is an essential element of living. Where there is no openness to learning there is no openness to life. Not that learning, as seen from the scriptures, is primarily an intellectual exercise. The best known group of learners in the Bible are the disciples. Their education was in life. It touched the whole of their existence: their beliefs, values, lifestyle, careers, relationships, hopes and fears, and their possessions. All this resulted from the coming of God's kingdom upon them.

They were learning a new way of looking at life, a new value system (expressed in the kingdom ethics of the Sermon on the Mount), and a new understanding of themselves (as children of God invited to call God *Abba*, Father). Instruction, even learning some things by heart, was involved, but much more besides. They learned as they watched, they learned as they related, they learned as they worked, they learned as they dared to show their ignorance and to ask questions.

This kingdom education was part of the way that God was (and still is today) redeeming his broken and fallen world. It involves bringing us to maturity 'in Christ' so that the image of God can be renewed in us as people. 'Salvation is, essentially considered,' says James Philip in his booklet *Christian Maturity*, 'the restoration of humanity to man.' 'The glory of God,' said St Irenaeus, 'is a man fully alive.'

The purpose of Christian learning is therefore to become mature as children of God and to reflect more of the family likeness. That is not a purely individualistic process: it involves us in being built into the community of believers. Nor is it just for the community of the faithful: our learning and maturing is for the world which God is committed to loving through his servant church. In short, the point of learning as Christians, and particularly for those in Christian leadership, is so that we may move towards maturity, together, in Christ, for the sake of the world. The goal, as we saw in the previous chapter, is that truth should be incarnate in us.

The Surprising Place

However, there is another meaning to the title 'The point of learning'. It can describe not just the purpose of learning but the place at which we learn. If we are committed to allowing God to take us as malleable metal onto the anvil of experience, we need to know where that will take place.

My conviction, which has arisen both from the study of scripture and from reflection on my own experience, is that for the Christian *learning takes place at the point of weakness*. Pain, failure and change, are at the heart of Christian learning; blessing, success and achievement are simply the fruit of that learning process. We are called, in Christ, to a through-death-to-life pattern of living expressed sacramentally by our passing through the waters of baptism, and ethically by our daily 'dying-to-live'.

All too easily we imagine that it is in the moment of success, achievement or victory that we learn most, yet this has not been so in my experience. It has been when things have not been going well and I have been up against it, feeling a failure and seeming to be trapped in a corner, that I have learned key lessons. It has been in dark moments that shafts of light have broken through and brought illumination. For this reason I believe that as Christians we need to have the courage to steer the ship of our lives into those dangerous waters of weakness, if we wish to learn and live. This has been the pattern of my learning about leadership. Five places of weakness stand out for me as areas that have been significant learning points.

First, is the place of ignorance. By this I mean the place where I feel I have little or nothing to offer. This is where I began in ministry, working with a group of inner-city young people in Manchester. Having had a public school, Cambridge University and southern upbringing, it was not to be expected that I would feel particularly at home in such a setting. Add to this culture shock the adjustment to being ordained and you can imagine how strange and bewildering it all seemed. Yet I had been designated the 'youth leader'. The only way to survive was to learn fast. I was enormously aided by a small group of particularly dedicated young evangelists who became – probably unknown to themselves – my trainers. I learned not simply about the urban youth culture, but about how to work with a team of gifted people.

Most of all I learned how to harness and blend gifted individuals into a coherent team. I also learned not to be afraid of working in a team where I was the layman and they were the experts. That was a lesson that has been repeated in several different situations since, notably in working on our church building project: and, more recently, in establishing an urban youth culture congregation. With both groups I have been in a leadership role while also knowing myself to be the joker in the pack – the one who has no qualifications to work with the particular materials (whether human or inanimate).

The leadership gift I had learned to bring in the face of such ignorance was the ability to steer things in the right direction. However, in each case I have had to work hard at catching up with the undoubted knowledge and expertise of those I was working with. It has meant learning to swim out of my depth and survive!

More recently we have been seeking to adjust to the fact that a church with over one thousand worshippers needs a leadership structure that is appropriate to its size. We have moved gradually from being like a family business to being more like a large firm, albeit one whose business is people. We need new structures.

We called together fifty of the senior leaders of the church to share some problems we had identified and some possible solutions. I was able to share the anger I had had to work through, that I was in this situation of handling a large organisation and yet the Church of England had given me nothing by way of initial training, or subsequent support, to prepare me for such a task. 'You need to remember,' I said, 'that I was trained in how to understand Habakkuk, not in how to develop management structures for a large church.'

I recount this because I did not, and still do not, find it easy to be in such a vulnerable place. Yet I have found not only that God, and his people, invariably come up with the answers, but also that such a situation provides me with an opportunity for rapid learning. That learning usually results from my asking someone in the know to educate and train me in the skills needed in this new situation. This requires some humility, but that is made easier by knowing that it is fatal to pretend you know answers when you are in the company of experts! You look much less stupid asking obvious questions than pretending you know answers. It is possible not just to survive, but to thrive, in such circumstances, and so the place of ignorance – which we naturally tend to avoid – can become the place of greatest growth.

Powerlessness
Second, is the place of impotence. It is difficult enough to cope with being ignorant about some technical area of expertise, but I have found more vulnerability in being powerless than in being ignorant – especially in the spiritual realm which others assume is my particular area of expertise.

My own experience of the renewing power of the Holy Spirit came about simply because I knew that my preaching was not having any effect, on me or the church. It was dry and theoretical, and sounded hollow. Yet that became probably the greatest learning point about God and his relationship to me that I have experienced outside of my initial conversion. In desperation I was driven to prayer, and found myself led to the parable of the importunate neighbour. The phrase that stood out with such clarity to me was the plea to his friend to give him some loaves 'because I have nothing to set before them' (Lk 11.6). I knew that was me: I had no bread to set before the church. I was not feeding them.

Yet it was this darkness and impotence that became the start of a process of learning about the presence and power of the Holy Spirit that continues to develop nearly twenty years later.

My entry into the healing ministry was also brought to birth in a place of impotence. An elderly member of the church had had five heart attacks and I went, with a couple from the church and the teenage sister of one of them, to take 'sick communion' – the evangelical equivalent of Last Rites. During the service I felt a strange warmth in my hands that puzzled me. I also felt an urge to lay hands on the woman and pray for healing. Then, reverting to my rational and professional mode, I realised how the young couple and the teenager would have their faith upset if I prayed and the woman did not get better. So I carried on my liturgical way, completed the service, and departed.

As we walked away from the house the teenager said, in a quiet confidential whisper, 'Should you do silly things when you think God is telling you to do them?' 'Like what?' I asked. She did not want to tell me so I said: 'Do you mean like praying for healing for that lady?' She blushed and knew she had been found out. Almost immediately I also blushed – for the same reason – I had been found out! After a quick word with the couple we turned around and went back in. We explained simply that we felt God was telling us to lay hands on her and pray for her. Was she willing for us to do that? She was: and so we did. We had been expecting the sixth and final heart attack any time – hence the communion. In fact she not only lived for another six or seven years, but during that time was able to break through from a 'works' mentality of earning salvation, to know in experience the grace of God's accepting love. Having begun her life as a housemaid she had an 'upstairs/downstairs' mentality in her approach to God. She knew she was in the household (of faith), but only so long as she behaved herself and was useful. In those remaining years of her life she came through to the knowledge that she really was a member of the family. She died secure in the experience of God's grace, rather than in hoping to achieve it by her behaviour.

That risk of faith was the door which opened the healing ministry for me. The learning point though was not some great experience of a miracle of healing: the healing was the consequence rather than the cause of my learning. Learning took place on the path outside when I turned round and went into what seemed to me to be a place of impotence. I learned in experience what God's word to the apostle Paul meant when he was told 'My strength is made perfect in weakness' (2 Cor 12.9).

Succeeding in Failure
Third, is the place of failure. This is always a difficult place

to enter, or to admit being in, either because it brings back memories of how we have failed before, or because, when we are leading others, we question whether they will be able to trust us to lead them when they know we have failed before.

Acknowledging failure was difficult for me, not least because after a successful education and a successful curacy (or so it seemed to me!) with a gifted incumbent, I had not come across much failure in my life.

Failure first stared me in the face with the collapse of all the uniformed organisations at St Thomas's – Cubs and Scouts, Brownies and Guides. This was compounded by the impending demise of the robed choir and the annual garden party (the highlight of the church's summer programme). Within the space of eighteen months all had gone. I had presided over the greatest collapse in church activities that the church had probably ever known. It had come about as the almost direct result of charismatic renewal. Looking back I can see that the old wineskins were leaking badly and needed to be replaced. In the purposes of God each one of those activities has been replaced with a modern equivalent which has become significantly more appropriate as a means of serving the church, and the local community, than the older forms would have been.

The problem was that neither of those things was known to me at the time. All I knew was that leadership was not forthcoming for them, and that despite considerable attempts to shore up these activities, they were about to collapse – on me! At just that time the scripture 'The Son does nothing of his own accord, but only what he sees the Father doing' (Jn 5.19) came to my attention. As I, and others involved in leadership, began to apply that to our situation we discerned that these collapsing organisations were not ways in which the Spirit was choosing to work at that time. Letting go, which included letting go of the expectations of some in the congregation, and of community expectations, was a costly step.

However, it was also a step that enabled me to learn much. One obvious lesson was that faith involves risk. Even more vital was the lesson that the church needs to be working on God's agenda and not on its own, or the community's, agenda. This step opened up the whole world of God's present-day ordering of his church. I learned to look for his plans and his purposes, and in looking back to see what he had been doing in the life of the church. Being willing to appear to fail was, for me, the opening of a window into the purposes of God. It even enabled me to become willing to return to areas where we had failed in the past.

One particular situation stands out. As the church grew throughout the seventies we began to realise that relationships were becoming very fragmented. With an average of nearly five hundred people in church every Sunday by the end of that decade, it was not possible to know, at least in any depth, most of the church. The sense of family was waning.

In an attempt to deal with this problem we divided our thirty-six supporting fellowship groups (home groups) into three 'areas'. They were based on geographical segments of the parish; three hopefully more manageable groupings, of a dozen or so groups each. This proved to be a valuable way of operating as a church. We held area get-togethers, area week-ends away, and area prayer meetings. Much was achieved in this way and the church continued to grow until by the mid-1980s we were up to an average of 650 people a Sunday in church.

However, the strains were showing in the whole 'areas' structure. We were discovering that most people could not retain a high level of commitment to all three levels (the home group, the 'area', and the whole church) at the same time. Moreover there was considerable overloading of the programme with each level really wanting people to attend a weekly meeting. In the end we decided that good though the 'areas' had been, we had to take courage in both hands and abandon them. It was costly and painful, made more so by the decision not to replace them with anything immediately. We decided rather to wait until we saw the way ahead. At least in the short term, it seemed as if we had failed.

It would have been much easier to have proposed an immediate replacement, but no such solution was evident. We accepted that the vacuum which would be created by stopping the areas would help us to understand what was to take their place. Such has been the case.

Two years later we introduced the idea of 'congregations' to the whole church. Essentially the idea was to turn each Sunday service into a pastoral unit with its own social, evangelistic, and pastoral groups and programmes. One of the great benefits of this was that we achieved the intermediate grouping that 'areas' provided without having any extra meetings. At the same time as introducing such 'congregations' we also divided the morning service into two; having the previous year established a youth culture congregation meeting at nine o'clock on Sunday evenings.

Those 'congregations' are now a vital part of the continuing growth of the church. Yet their conception depended on both letting go of something that was good but not right, and also being willing to return to an area in the life of the church where we felt as if we had failed in the past. They were the fruit of the courage to return to the place of failure. Growth in leadership ability may often require such a return journey at some stage.

Learning in the place of failure also involves the faith and courage to admit when we have got something wrong. I have learned over the years that one of the most liberating expressions of faith is to say *'It's not working.'* A great dam of guilt and frustration can be drained by doing so, and in its wake a tide of creativity is often released. Sadly though, a false notion of faith makes us think that 'keeping the show on the road' and keeping up appearances ('positive thinking'), is the supreme expression of faith. It just is not so. Admitting that something is not working involves a greater degree of faith: a confidence that, in God, answers we cannot find can yet be discovered.

This willingness, reluctant and costly though it may be, to acknowledge that something is not working, lay behind many of the incidents I have already mentioned in this chapter. It was a significant factor in abandoning uniformed organisations, a robed choir, and our garden party. I am not advocating that others should necessarily follow our course in abandoning similar activities in their situations: rather, my concern is that when something is not achieving its intended goal we should ask sharp and objective questions, and be willing to consider the option of abandoning the venture.

However, the greatest, and most painful, admission of something not working was at a time of crisis and shaking (to which I devoted a chapter of *In the Crucible*) within the staff team. We had set out to achieve what we called 'corporate leadership' but it had developed into something that was a caricature of the idea. We spent many hours, and not a few tears, trying to make it work, and very nearly split the church in the attempt. The relief when I dared to admit to myself that 'it's not working' was vast and memorable. When, in the goodness of God, we had come through that turbulent time into calmer waters and had seen the growth of the church picking up after three years of plateau, it was tempting to write the whole experience off as wasted time. Yet, here again, I now see that the growth of St Thomas's that has taken place since then is the direct consequence of facing our failure and admitting that what we were doing was not working.

A Risky Business

Fourth, is the place of risk. I can now see, looking back, that every significant step forward in the life of the church has involved risk.

Stepping into charismatic renewal ran the real risk of splitting the church. Launching into what was to become a building project costing two-thirds of a million pounds looked like a sure path to bankruptcy and folly. Involvement in a local ecumenical project with the local Baptist church seemed like giving away everything that had been sacrificially won, and like changing a winning team for an unknown quantity. Launching the urban culture nine o'clock service looked a crazy thing to do, with little chance of holding it and the rest of the church together as one. Developing every service as a separate congregation seemed another way of ensuring permanent division. With both the nine o'clock service and the starting of congregations as pastoral units still only relatively recent, we do not yet know for sure that they are going to work. As I write we are still in the high-risk phase.

Something I find most difficult about risk-taking is that every time the church grows we seem to sense God's call to another step of faith. Yet each time the risk is bigger; and the stakes become higher. However, these events are points of growing and learning for the whole church. Indeed, without the risks having been taken there would be little or no story to tell. Along the way I have learned something about faith which has surprised me.

Initially I had thought that faith was the absolute certainty which enables us to take the risk out of living. I now understand it to be God's gift which enables us to enter into risks with no certainty about the outcome other than that we will find God faithful.

At one point in our building project, I felt as if I had come to the end of my faith – and said so to God. Over the previous three or so years we had given £300,000. That had been the anticipated target. However, due to inflation and rising costs, we then still needed more than that again – and within the next six months. Immediately after I expressed my feelings of despair to God, I sensed his undergirding presence and the familiar words from the Anglican funeral service (perhaps not an especially encouraging source!) came to my mind: 'Underneath are the everlasting arms'. I was at the limit of my faith. In that moment God was saying to me, 'I have seen your faith, but now let me show you my faithfulness'.

That is all the confidence and certainty we ever need. By a series of miracles we actually saw the target reached after that, at the rate of £2,000 a day for the last one hundred days of the project. The fact is that if as leaders we take risks we may well get some things wrong. However, if we do not take any risks we will certainly not get much right.

On the Frontiers
Finally, learning takes place at the frontiers. This is where I see that God wants leaders to live: at the frontiers where faith engages with experience which does not match our hopes; where love is poured out to a broken and often unbelieving and unaccepting world; where obedience challenges all the comforts and securities in which the culture around us puts its faith. Life at these frontiers is risky and full of uncertainty. There are no sure maps or guarantees of success: just the promise of God's presence. But this is where the Spirit is at work, where we learn, and where God is most readily encountered. This is where the kingdom of God is revealed. For this reason it is in these places that the Christian leader needs to be found.

A Modern Example
One modern example of this cross-and-resurrection pattern of

learning in the place of weakness was a great inspiration to me in the early days of experiencing renewal. It was the work of Graham Pulkingham in the early 1970s. Graham was the Rector of the downtown Church of the Redeemer parish in Houston, Texas. Faced with a local community of people in often desperate human need he had the courage to face his, and the church's, failure.

In a moving passage from his book *They Left Their Nets* he tells the story of his struggles.

> By then it was late spring and the parish was already on its last legs; like a stricken bird fluttering at a cat's play, its good works were spent in wasted efforts. The doors to the gym were padlocked again, and the onslaught ceased. I was in despair. Everything that was offered had been despised, and finally the church withdrew.
>
> But how could I retreat? My soul was stuck fast in extraordinary compassion for the neighbourhood and its struggling folk. Perhaps the church had failed to call forth the kingdom of God's love, but during the past several months something in me had been irreversibly altered and I refused to back off . . . I took the burden of it into a lonely basement chapel which for six weeks, from Ash Wednesday to Easter, became my tomb of despair.
>
> It was in that lonely chapel during Lent that I became a visionary. There revelations I received were not flights of fancy or mere daydreams, nor were they conclusions drawn from rapidly reasoned processes . . . In the unveiling of two stark future moments I visualised the church of Eastwood as it was to be – a loving, sharing, serving, community of praise and thanksgiving, and I saw the ministry, or more particularly I saw my own ministry as it was to be . . .
>
> Out of my lonely suffering was emerging a new hope, not a new self-image: the possibility of authority . . . given directly by the author of life Himself, an authenticating power to overcome opposing works of darkness and stop their destruction at the well-spring or subdue them at the flood. It involved a mysterious endowment of power to impart life for death, health for sickness, and freedom for bondage.

Out of that lonely and painful pilgrimage came a work of great grace through the establishing of caring community households in which costly love, and the healing power of God, were released. Out of that searching came the international ministry of the Fisherfolk worship group whose impact on the worship of much church life in the Western world is still with us. Graham was a man who had the courage to face weakness, own it, and encounter God in its depths.

Embracing the Cross

When the story of what has happened at St Thomas's is told it sounds immensely exciting. At times it has felt like that. However, for most of the time it has seemed very unlike that. Indeed out of it has come my conviction that if we are to know resurrection life and power and blessing in our service of God, there is no other route than going the way of the Cross. This is the only point of learning for us: the only way that truth will become incarnated in us and in our leadership.

It will involve us in travelling to places of weakness, impotence, failure, risk, and the frontiers of the kingdom of God. It is here – not in our 'successes' or achievements – but in our pain, in our discontent, and in our choosing to be vulnerable that true learning takes place. Out of that comes the fruit and blessing which God alone gives. We express our faith by being willing to enter – indeed to pitch our tent and live – in the place of weakness.

This may appear to be a vastly more threatening approach to learning the skills of leadership than through academic study, and our defence mechanism may well seek to prevent us from going along such a route. Ultimately, though, I believe that it is the only way into the real fruit and blessing God desires to bring about in our lives, as well as in the lives of those he has called us to lead.

Chapter Three

A FRAMEWORK FOR LEARNING

We have seen so far that the key to growth in leadership is a matter of allowing God to write his truth in us as people so that we become part of the message that he intends to communicate to others. For this to happen we have to make ourselves available to God as malleable metal on the anvil of experience. We can dare to do this because we know that the divine Blacksmith is motivated wholly by love. We can trust him even in the pain. And that is where we will frequently find that we are – in a place of weakness, learning from God. But the question still remains, how do we learn? How can we hear what God is saying, and allow him to reshape us; rather than jump to the wrong conclusions or hide from the testing that is upon us? The answer to these questions will occupy the next two chapters, before we can turn to the practical outworking of learning from experience.

As I have reflected on my own faltering steps in the art of learning from experience, I came to see that there was a framework within which this learning was taking place. There was a regularity and shape to the learning that has enabled me to check for direction, and get my bearings in the midst of the storms of life. I now see that this framework has been crucial to my own experience of learning.

Though the framework is conceptual, I have made a model (below) in an attempt to demonstrate physically how the principle functions. In a square piece of wood I cut a triangular hole and at each corner of the triangle I screwed a hook. Taking a large wooden curtain ring I looped three rubber bands to it,

A framework for learning

looping the other end of each band over one of the hooks. Onto the curtain ring I put a drawing of a man on a small piece of acetate sheet so that he appears at the centre of the triangle; held in tension by the three rubber bands.

This model gives a description of the three factors in the incarnational learning process which, if kept in balance, can hold us in the centre of God's purposes. These three elements are *intuition*, *analysis* and *inspiration*. This chapter will consider the first two of these elements (intuition and analysis). The following chapter will address the third factor (inspiration).

Intuition
The trouble with my favourite television programme is that it is only shown once every four or five years. I would trade all other viewing for that time when I can settle down into the early hours of the morning to see what happens as the general election results come in.

Imagine then my horror when someone, confessing to have been deeply involved in black magic, appeared at church during the week in which a general election took place. This twenty-year-old girl proceeded to take up much of each day of that week as more and more confessions of gruesome rituals were laid before us. I could see what was coming. I knew I would have to make the supreme sacrifice – to forego watching the election results. It was well past midnight before our daily session was over, and I was in no mood to catch up with what was happening. But that night's work, I thought, had uncovered the last and worst of this story – she had been involved in child sacrifice. Reluctantly, she agreed to meet a solicitor next day to tell all and face the consequences. So my sacrifice seemed worth it.

Election night, however, was the last we ever saw of her. To this day I do not know whether the story was true, but I am as convinced as I need to be that it was simply an elaborate way of seeking attention. All of us involved admitted, on reflection, that we had not really believed the story. Each felt there was something not right about how she had told it, but had held back, fearing that we might be seen to be unloving or unspiritual.

It had taken the best part of a week to learn something that was expressed in words I have always remembered – *trust your humanity*. I resolved to take notice of my God-given instincts rather than to suppress and ignore them. When, ten years later, we were in a serious leadership crisis, I recognised afterwards that again I had failed to trust my instinctive feeling for what was going on. Indeed, most of my worst mistakes have involved this failing.

The first element in the framework of the learning process is therefore the intuitive exercise of our own instincts and insights. The dictionary definition of intuition is 'the power of the mind by which it immediately perceives the truth of things without reasoning or analysis'. Some of us will have a better feel for situations than others, but where our feel is blurred and poor we will find that it will develop if we recognise that it is a God-given resource to be exercised.

There is certainly a considerable risk involved. My instincts and judgement could well be shown, by subsequent events, to have been faulty. They are certainly not infallible. Yet ignoring them has frequently ended in my doing more harm than would have been done if I had trusted them. As long as the other two factors – inspiration and analysis – are allowed to play their full role I can be confident that intuition need never lead to self-delusion.

Intuition is an ability to see below the surface of events and to feel what is truly taking place. It is like a sixth sense. In fact we often use the words of the other senses to describe it. 'Now I *see* what is going on', 'I *smell* trouble here', 'It all *sounds* a bit dubious to me', 'It leaves an unpleasant *taste* in my mouth, all the same'.

All of us have a feel for a situation and task. Often I find that it is most evidently at work when the outward events point in a contrary direction to what I am feeling. It may be that someone is saying something valid about the life or state of the church, but I sense discomfort about their motives. There is power-seeking or manipulation taking place. What the person is saying may well be valid, but I know I must be on full alert in such a situation. Is this not what Jesus was doing when we read, 'Jesus would not entrust himself to them . . . for he knew what was in a man' (Jn 2.24).

I have learned to heed, to face and admit, what I feel about a situation. Intuition is an important means of reading a situation. Recognising its importance has enabled me to integrate that part of my make-up into the task of leadership. It has also enabled me to trust my instincts even when I have no particular reasons for taking, or refusing to take, some action. My responses (as well as my reason) need to be opened before God for him to correct or overrule, but they need also to be faced, owned, acknowledged and trusted.

Honestly facing his feelings was an important part of what Jesus was doing in Gethsemane. Few preachers or commentators on the prayer of Jesus in Gethsemane seem to have seen the

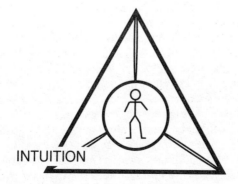

Intuition in the framework for learning

amazing honesty of the prayer. Here was Jesus, the eternal Son of God, who had freely chosen from all eternity to come to earth and die for man. Now, as he faces that moment, we hear not some high and gloriously inspired prayer but Jesus saying to his Father, 'I don't want to go through with it: find me a way out.' Jesus does not end his prayer there. Prayer for him was dialogue with God in which he learned to see things differently, to change and grow and make choices, because he was engaged in a living relationship with the Father. Nonetheless, this was his starting point. He spoke honestly about how he felt.

My experience is that, when I face my feelings and reactions and bring them into the open before God, I am then able to be much more discerning about the situation. Sometimes I see God's way leading along the line of my feelings, but at other times – as in Gethsemane – God calls us, after having faced and owned our feelings, to lay them on one side and choose a way that seems contrary. This is never easy, but incarnating the will of God is vital if we are ever to lead others more fully into his purposes.

Many steps forward in the life of the church have come through intuition, before arguments in favour of such a development have emerged. Intuition functions as an early warning system. It alerts the leader to problems and opportunities that lie ahead.

After returning to the re-ordered church building at the end of 1980, we were faced with two decisions about how to handle our time in the coming year. The possibility of forming a united church with the local Baptist church had already been explored at an initial level. Intuition had alerted me that we were not going to be able to deal with all the detailed work and emotional upheaval during the building project. Reluctantly we agreed to put the whole matter on 'hold' for over a year. That proved to be the right timing.

However, we also discussed whether we should make that first year back in the building a 'year of evangelism'. There were many arguments in favour: here was a new beginning and a new opportunity. It was to make space for others that we had launched into the building project. The church needed a new focus for its life. Yet my intuition told me that the church was tired and likely to experience anti-climax after the great event.

Moreover there were many changes in the leadership ahead of us that year. I allowed the arguments to overrule my intuition. It was not a good decision. Little was achieved evangelistically, other than a sense of guilt at failing to achieve an over-ambitious programme of visiting, and we missed a great opportunity to learn how to rest and relax in our worship and faith, rather than always be out achieving.

Ignoring intuition, both mine and also that of others, was also the primary cause of the biggest crisis we have experienced – to date! The story of the time of shaking is told in detail in *In the Crucible*. Several people had alerted me to the seeds of our problems two years before they surfaced in a way no one could escape. By ignoring those feelings of unease, we stored up a major crisis for ourselves which could have been defused much more easily if we had acted earlier.

Analysis
The second element in the framework of learning is the rational and logical work of analysis. It involves the willingness to put thought and effort into clear thinking. Seeking to move in the realm of faith often tempts us to assume that we know the answers without having to think the issues through. On occasions I have seen this at work in the counselling ministry where, because a Christian has confidence in Jesus as God's ultimate answer to man's need, he acts as though he knew the answer before he had even heard the questions being asked by the person being counselled. Faith then becomes the excuse for not thinking. However, God has given us minds and they are part of what we bring into the learning situation for him to work in and through.

Being willing to analyse how effective we have been pastorally in the area of leadership involves faith – indeed it is an expression of unbelief not to dare to face the facts. It speaks of unwillingness to expose ourselves to how God would wish to re-shape us. So then, we have a second element in our framework for learning.

By 'analysis' I mean all that is involved in understanding what is happening in the development of a group or church. Analysis might take place through the use of statistics, an understanding of the sociology of groups, or the rationale behind the church

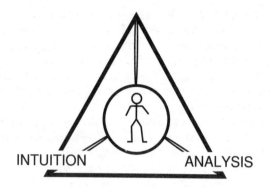

Intuition and analysis in the framework for learning

growth movement. Many different disciplines can help us to analyse what is happening around us, but each involves the disciplined application of our minds to work out what is happening and why some things work well and others do not.

Later chapters will give a number of different analytical tools which I have found of enormous help in understanding what has been happening in the church and which have made a major contribution to the quality and strength of the solutions which have been discovered.

One illustration will suffice here. Shortly after the church's experience of charismatic renewal we felt the call of God to develop small home groups within the church. In the process of reading about such groupings, I came across the church growth analysis of the three different levels of groupings every believer benefits from being involved in.

The first level is in a unit of *celebration* in which people are inspired by the big event. The ultimate example of this is a visit by an international figure, such as the Pope or Billy Graham, which can draw Christians from many churches into a great event sometimes involving millions of people. For those actually present, they are never-to-be-forgotten experiences which fire the believers' imagination and remind them of the central truths of the faith. Their effectiveness works on the principle of 'the bigger the better'. Relationship with other people who are there is of little or no importance. 'I was there' is what matters.

At the other end of the scale, every believer will benefit by being part of a *cell* group: a small, secure, home-based face-to-face grouping of eight to twenty or so. This cannot compete with the celebration, but it provides what that cannot: secure relationships where attention can be given to my hopes and fears, needs and opportunities. It enables every member to feel valued, and to be helped to grow as a person and in faith.

Between these two groups is the grouping of a *congregation*. By this is meant a grouping of one hundred and fifty to two hundred and fifty. This grouping is held together by relationships but has many more resources than the cell. It will have teachers and musicians and people able to work with children and young people – all of which skills may be missing in the small group.

Equipped with this analytical tool we were able to understand what was going on in the life of the church. We saw that we had started with a congregation (the Sunday services) to which we had added cell groups – our supporting fellowships. However, these small groups had caused the church to grow to the point where the Sunday services were becoming much more like celebration events in which people were drawn together by the experience rather than through relationships. As a result we realised that having begun with a congregation we had ended up with a celebration unit and with cells.

What was needed was to build back the congregational unit into the life of the church. We did this first by grouping the fellowship groups together in geographical 'areas'. That enabled further growth to take place, but intuition and analysis both led us to the conclusion that this was not the long term way ahead. In due course we identified the Sunday services as the most natural congregational unit and have sought to develop them as such.

The use of analytical tools by themselves is as dangerous as operating purely on intuition. But there are many with which it is vital we become acquainted if we are to develop a fully rounded and mature leadership ability.

Working Together
Experience has taught me that, important though intuition and analysis are, something more sophisticated is needed than ensuring that we have both. They need to find not just shared

accommodation in our minds, but a marriage in our personalities. We need to learn how to integrate them in our experience of leadership. Sometimes it is analysis which identifies a problem and intuition which uncovers an answer. Sometimes it is intuition which produces an idea and analysis which establishes a rationale for the idea. Most frequently I have made an intuitive discovery and then, through subsequent analysis, seen the rational basis for it. I have thereby come to understand at the intellectual level what God first gave in an experiential way.

An example comes to mind from the area of counselling skills. Part of my seeking after God, that led to encountering the Holy Spirit in a more intimate and personal way, was the awareness that people did not seem to look to me for counselling and help with personal problems. It was not so much that I needed to be needed, but that I knew it to be a sign that I was not truly feeding the flock. The uncomfortable conclusion was that I had nothing to set before them and they sensed it enough not to come to me for such food.

Very soon after experiencing the fresh coming of the Spirit, I had a desperate phone call from someone at seven o'clock in the morning, telling me that her husband had attempted to commit suicide and asking me to come. I went as soon as possible. The man was out of danger, but having taken an overdose, was still very drowsy, so I agreed to return that evening. I spent a restless day in prayer. The thrust of my praying was 'Lord, you know I have longed to meet the real needs of hurting people, but it is not fair for a couple in such need to be guinea pigs for my learning: it is just not a responsible way for you to act!' However, that evening my wife Ann and I were there on the doorstep offering help – though we were at a loss to know what we could do.

God, however, met the couple with much grace that night. Repentance, forgiveness, dealing with the hurts and sense of failure that had sparked the desperate cry for help, were all touched by God's gentle mercy and goodness. Ann and I came away marvelling at what we had been privileged to witness. Rather like midwives we felt that what had been achieved was so little of our doing, yet we were also aware of the stages God led us to take this couple through.

When, in subsequent years, I was undertaking some counselling training, what struck me was how right Ann and I had been in the way that we had handled that situation, despite the fact that we felt totally out of our depth from start to finish. That training was a great help in enabling us to analyse and understand what had happened, in order to prepare for parallel situations. But it came after the actual experience of that ministry. The starting point was God's use of our intuition through which to lead us.

A similar pattern was evident when we began our home groups. Intuitively we had decided that we should work on a multiplication-by-division pattern. Each group would be encouraged to grow to around sixteen and then to divide into two smaller groups and begin to grow again. In this way we started with three groups and had grown to thirty-six within eight years. Only later on did I discover an analysis of what was going on that gave me a rational basis for such an approach.

An in-depth survey of the church four years after we had started the groups was carried out by the Rev David Wasdell of the Urban Church Project. His central thesis, the result of the analysis of a vast number of church statistics, was that churches fail to grow primarily because they do not have the structures to enable growth to take place. He had come to the conclusion that small units which grew in number by division was the way forward. It was a great encouragement to discover that there were good reasons for what we were doing.

Further confirmation of our intuitive decision came from a member of the church who was working in biological research. She made the point that cells have a central nucleus and an outer wall. As the cell moves towards multiplication there is first an elongation of the cell walls from a circular to an elliptical shape. Then a second nucleus begins to emerge like the two focal points of an ellipse. Later on a thin membrane starts to develop between the two nuclei. That gradually thickens until each nucleus has a complete outer shell around it. At that point the two cells break away to become independent cells. God had led us to do in our cell groups what he already did in his cells!

In this process of growth by division, we began with an intuitive response to the situation. Then came sociological support for such an approach, enhanced by a biological picture of how cells multiply in nature. This was finally enriched by seeing – at the spiritual level – how Jesus himself was involved in the same experience as he went the way of the cross. These all became tools to help us analyse and understand what was happening with our groups.

A similar pattern of intuition followed by analysis was evident when in 1987 we made each Sunday service into a pastoral unit by making it a congregation in its own right. One of the questions which had to be resolved was how to structure the leadership. We had decided that each congregation would have its own leadership team, but how would they relate to one another? And how would the specialist ministries like missionary support, worship teams, and our work with children and young people, relate to those leadership groups? It was quite a puzzle, but as I thought about it the picture of the warp and weft of material came to my mind and with it the awareness that that is how material gains its strength. Out of this came the idea of having a net-like pattern of leadership relationships as illustrated below.

To me it was an entirely original thought. As far as I was aware no one had ever thought of this way of handling leadership structures before. Aware of this I said in the written presentation to the church council: 'Will this warp and weft in the leader-

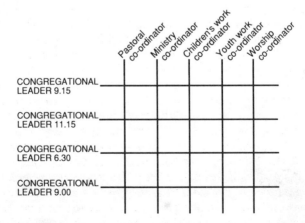

Our present leadership structure

ship structures make for twice the strength, or double the hassle?' After two years of working this way my answer is 'Both!'

Since that time, however, I have discovered that this is a tried and tested way of handling leadership in large organisations, called a leadership matrix. Books and articles I have read about such a pattern say that it is very tempting to avoid handling leadership this way in a large organisation where authority is shared around to a considerable degree, but it proves to be essential. That has been a great encouragement to us to press on – through the problems. Intuition gave the lead, and analysis then supplied the back-up understanding and rational basis which helped us to see more clearly what we were doing.

Personal Integration

My present understanding of the relationship between intuition and analysis is that this pattern, of intuition leading the way with analysis supporting, is how the relationship between these two elements works for me. I am an intuitive person and have had to learn to exercise the discipline of analysis and to discover how these two elements can co-operate in leadership. Some others might be much more analytical and would find that that aspect was to the fore. They will then have to work hard to give recognition to intuition and allow it space to contribute to their leadership, if they are to achieve a balanced and mature leadership style. This is simply the outworking of the principle of learning happening in the place of weakness. For the intuitive leaders to develop their intuition and the analytical leaders to develop their rational skills, is not sufficient. Rather, both have to learn to move into their area of weakness (not least by balancing their team work with people who are strong where they are weak).

However it is done, a marriage between intuition and analysis needs to take place in everyone who desires to mature as a person and as a leader. Such a marriage can have an amazingly creative effect. Einstein is an unlikely model for Christian leaders, but the following story told by Morton Kelsey, in *Encounter with God*, gloriously demonstrates the creativity released when these two elements are brought together in one person:

Einstein's reported remark to Jung is the classic description. Asked if he had to work very hard to produce his equations, Einstein smiled. 'Oh, no,' he said, 'I meditate and the numbers dance before me.'

There is a deeper reason, however, for using the marriage analogy to describe the relationship between intuition and analysis, for they point us to the masculine and feminine characteristics present in our make-up as humans. As I have reflected on this, the writing of two people, both of whom have greatly contributed to my understanding of the faith, have spoken to me. First, Paul Tournier, in *The Gift of Feeling*, writes:

> The fact is that the complementarity of the sexes is more than an external harmony between two distinct beings, man and woman, in marriage and in their social relationships. It is also an interior harmony within each of us, both men and women, between our masculine and our feminine tendencies . . . C. G. Jung used the terms *animus* for the masculine tendency present in the mind of the woman, and *anima* for the feminine tendency present in that of the man.

Second, C. S. Lewis in a letter he wrote to a sister Penelope (quoted by Leanne Payne in her book *Crisis in Masculinity*), said:

> 'There ought spiritually to be a man in every woman and woman in every man. And how horrid ones who haven't got it are: I can't bear a "man's man" and "woman's woman".'

If this is so, then learning to integrate the masculine and feminine attributes needs to take place in each leader (of either sex) and in all leadership teams, whose composition needs to reflect this balance and integration. In this way we individually, and as a community, are coming to the maturity for which God has made us, and for the fruitfulness and creativity which result from the union of the masculine and feminine.

It expresses also the outworking of God's purposes of taking leaders onto the anvil. It is not just to hammer out impurities, but to temper and strengthen the metal so that it can have the richness of characteristics which hitherto have lain dormant. God takes us onto the anvil primarily because of what he wants to give to us and add to our wholeness. However, the best is yet to come, for all we have considered so far has been how the *animus* and *anima* can be united in one person, and in one team. Now we must turn our attention to how our humanity can be harnessed to the mind and purposes and action of God.

Chapter Four

DISCOVERING GOD'S AGENDA

I love the story of an ecumenical dialogue between (in the version I as an Anglican first heard it) a Methodist minister and a Catholic priest. At the end of an enjoyable time together the Methodist minister decided that it was time to go. He stood up, shook the priest by the hand and said: 'Ah well, I suppose we must be getting back to the Lord's work: you doing it in your way and me doing it in his!' That remark may not score very high on humility, but it does point to what the heart of all ministry should be – finding and doing the will of God. Christian leadership is about discovering what God is wanting to do in me and with me and through me. It is for the coming of *his* kingdom, and the doing of *his* will that we pray. For that prayer to be answered we need to be able to hear God's voice and discern his will in our situation.

This is why the third and key factor in the framework for learning is therefore *inspiration*, or our knowing the call and purposes of God. This is how the supernatural or divine side of leadership contributes to and shapes the human side. It is inspiration which both stretches intuition and analysis and enables them to fulfil their role of holding the leader in the centre of God's will. When all three elements are functioning properly then all experience can be harnessed to the furtherance of God's will both in the leader and in the group being led. So now, in this chapter, we turn to this third and most vital element in the framework for learning.

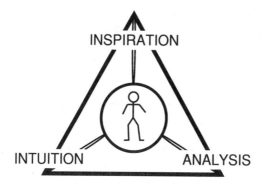

Intuition, analysis, and inspiration in the framework for learning

Inspiration

Knowing God is what Christianity is all about. At the heart of that knowing is the hearing of his word and the discovery of his will. As previously recounted, it took me some time to realise that it was God's agenda which I was called to work on – not mine. This required a commitment to work at learning to hear God's voice and to discern his mind and will. Though I still do not consider myself very proficient at it, I certainly now know this to be what Christian leadership is about – taking people into the will of God. The knowledge of that will comes about by the inspiration of the Holy Spirit and for me it has happened in four very different ways.

First, God's direction has come through a living dialogue with the scriptures. By this I mean the process of looking at our experience and practices in the light of what God says through his word, and allowing what we do to be changed and conformed to what God has said. This is the ultimate form of expository preaching in which a community begins to live the truth revealed to it through the scriptures. There are few more powerful or holy things on this earth than a body of believers who have moved from grasping God's word to being grasped and shaped by it. Our life as a church has been deeply affected by this process of dialogue with the word of God particularly affecting our motivation in giving and service.

55

In the area of giving, our building project put us firmly onto the anvil of experience, as a result of which the truth of the scriptures was hammered into us as a community. In preaching on the primary texts on giving in 2 Corinthians 8 and 9, we soon realised that Paul was as concerned about the motivation as about the amount of the church's giving. He pointed the Corinthians to the experience of the Macedonians and wrote about how God's grace had been evident in them. He was not drawing attention to how generous the Macedonians were, but how evidently they had experienced God's grace. He then followed up that testimony by teaching about the motivation he was looking for:

> Each man should give what he has decided in his heart to give, not reluctantly or under compulsion, for God loves a cheerful giver.

The result of our seeking to live in the truth of this text was a decision (contrary to natural inclination) not to set any personal targets for giving for individuals, but rather to encourage them to pray and discover God's will for them. I am convinced that the remarkable generosity of the church was the direct consequence of our having built our practice of giving around the principles of God's word.

Later on we were to go through a similar process of reflection on the scriptures about motivation for Christian service. Soon after my renewing experience of the Holy Spirit I was disturbed by a verse from Isaiah 58 which says: 'On the day of your festivals . . . you exploit all your workers' (Is 58.3). It left me feeling very uncomfortable. I came to realise that the discomfort was because, at least to some extent, I was seeking to get things to happen in the church in order to satisfy a need in me for achievement and recognition. I realised that this was no way to build the kingdom or 'work the works of God'. I had to let go of the need to succeed and achieve, and allow God to give success or failure, praise or criticism – as he chose. Out of this dialogue came the conviction that the ministry of the church should be built on grace: the free giving of service in response to the grace and call of God, and not out of moral pressure or duty induced by the vicar.

It has been a difficult path to tread. Faith has had to be exercised when no one has sensed the call of God to do some vital work. Yet we have often seen so much fruitfulness when the person leading a particular part of the work is doing it out of a sense of call and openness to God, not out of a sense of duty. Such blessing is just one example of the fruit that is borne from engaging in living dialogue with the word of God.

Second, God's agenda for me as a person has often been the preparation for his purposes for the church. This was certainly so in the case of charismatic renewal. It came about because of the spiritual hunger and unreality I was going through at the time. Furthest from *my* thoughts was what was next on the agenda for the church. I was simply desperate about my lack of living touch with God and was devoting myself to finding answers in the spiritual darkness I was experiencing. By the time I had come through these months of searching, I discovered that a sizeable group of the church had meanwhile begun to speak in tongues and do other things that seemed strange at the time.

Since then I have been able to see where my journey with God has been intersecting with the journey that others are making. It is all part of believing that God knew what he was doing when he called me to this particular job. In fact, during this period of charismatic renewal and upheaval there were some who clearly thought that I was no longer a suitable person to lead the church and were quite ready to suggest who should be called in to 'sort out the mess'.

At that time a thought came into my mind during my daily prayer time. It was rather startling in its bluntness. The thought was simply that 'You are the best vicar of Crookes in the world!' As I puzzled over that seemingly proud remark (particularly strange because I was so often tempted to join in the questioning of others about my suitability) a further phrase came to my mind as commentary on the first. This was: '. . . because you are the only one I have called to do the job at present!' I have taken this to be from God, not least because subsequently it has led neither to pride nor to over-confidence in myself as God's answer to everything. Rather it has enabled me to take risks for him in the belief that the convictions he gives are to be acted upon for the church, and are likely to fit in with what he is doing already in the lives of other church members.

Third, there have been clear prophetic words that have given direction for the life of the church. Such was the case in the establishing of fellowship groups in the early 1970s. We had come as a church to give thanks for God's blessing on a gift day when, in answer to our prayer for 'not less than £1,250', we had seen over £3,000 given on the day. In the midst of that thanksgiving a picture of the church as a building site came to my mind, and with it came these words:

> *I am building my church in this place. I am not calling you now to gather more stones, for they are all here on the site. But they are scattered and separate. I will build my church with these stones, but for this to happen they must be joined to each other, cemented together in love. As that happens, those who are hurt and needy will be drawn to this place. They will find shelter from the storm, and strength and refreshment to go out to serve me in the world. But, remember, those stones must be built together, cemented together in love, if my church is to be built.*

A similar prophetic word was the seed that brought to birth the nine o'clock service in 1986. I had been involved in setting up a John Wimber Signs and Wonders Conference in Sheffield in the autumn of 1985. Following that visit we had a team from the Vineyard churches to lead three evening meetings at St Thomas's. On the final evening we had one thousand people crammed into the building. Steve Nicholson, a young Vineyard pastor from inner-city Chicago, spoke and then asked people to stand as he invited the Holy Spirit to come in power on the whole gathering. Then all heaven, and yes all hell, had been let loose. Screaming and weeping swirled all around. A couple of dozen or more people fell to the ground under the power and sense of the presence of God. I was in the middle of a group of black-clad young people in their early twenties. They had been sitting on the floor at the front of the meeting and the Spirit of God seemed to be focused upon them. I was catching bodies and laying as many of them down as I could. However, the place was so crowded I ended up like a true pillar of the church with several of the young people slumped against me.

With my mind fully occupied with the immediate and physical problems of this dramatic ending to the meeting a thought came into my mind. In fact I can only describe it as if it was there and I stumbled across it. I cannot recall the actual words, maybe there were not any, but I knew in a profound way that God was wanting to add two or three hundred such young people to the church in a short space of time, in months rather than years.

Out of that moment of inspiration has come a new congregation with a radical worship style geared to the urban youth culture. Within two years we had seen over two hundred added to the church from a totally un-churched culture. The prophetic word came in a flash: its outworking – I hope – will outlast my lifetime. Wonderful though it is to be part of that work of God, I would not be honest if I did not also acknowledge the costs of such a radical move. It has meant an enormous expenditure of time to bring it about. At the heart of this congregation is a group of eighteen dedicated people. Ten have paid employment, and by sharing 'a common purse' that makes it possible for the other eight to work full-time in the congregation. Eight full-time workers in any congregation will have a profound effect: the cost is simple living and a shared lifestyle.

The development of this congregation has also meant considerable costs for the rest of the church. Great patience and forbearance and endless hours of consultation and discussion have been required. The wear and tear on our buildings has been considerable, as well as the strain on our budget. There still remain tension points in which the clash of two cultures is taking place. The human cost has been considerable on both sides, and yet God is at work fulfilling the prophecy given on that dramatic night.

Although this aspect of inspiration is the most striking, it is important to say that significant guidance from God has come to us only about three times in this clear 'prophetic' way. Each time it has launched us into powerful new developments that we would probably never have come near to without such a strong directive; but they have been the exception rather than the rule. Much more gradual and gentle means of discovering God's agenda are our more normal experience.

Fourth, God's inspiration has come to us through prayerful reflection on what God is saying to us through our circumstances. The launching of the major building project in 1976 came about this way. We had resisted thoughts about re-ordering the buildings because we had sensed that our being cemented together in love was God's primary call to us. However, one of the fruits of that unity was a greater vision and eagerness to serve the community. Increasingly we became aware of how unsuitable were our buildings (church, hall, and partial use of the adjoining church school) for the new patterns of worship and fellowship that had developed, as well as for our fresh desire to serve the local community.

Only after resisting plans initially, and then exploring alternatives, were we finally driven back to the conclusion not only that a major re-ordering was right, but that this was the moment to act. The phrase which described the vision was 'bringing all our buildings onto one site in a multi-purpose, flexible use, maintenance-free building'. At one level it was simply the fruit of careful thought and planning, yet undergirding it – and it was this that convinced me that the time to act had come – was the sense that *now* was God's moment. Intuition and analysis were vital preparation but what I can only describe as an inner conviction was the key to action.

The Quakers have a saying about 'follow your peace'; and at that time peace meant ceasing from simply thinking and considering alternatives. It meant a call to action. Thus came about the launching of a five-year building project which was to have a profound effect on the spiritual and material life of every member of the church. Certainly, it was the result of human thought, but far more importantly, it was a plan impregnated with life from God through the sense that this was now *his* will, and *his* moment for action.

The uniting of St Thomas's with Crookes Baptist church in 1982 came about in a similar way. Due to the building project, we had to move out of the church for nearly two years. The local Baptist church generously took us in. They moved into their church hall and allowed us to use the main church building. It was a squash to get everyone in, but we managed it. We worked well together as two churches but had little or no thought of any lasting relationship after the longed-for return to the new building. It was a chance remark that I made to the then Baptist minister which took root and eventually was to produce the lasting fruit of a fully fledged local ecumenical project at St Thomas's. Thus the two denominations were united in one worshipping community that functions to all intents and purposes as one church.

Here again, as in the building project, it was intuition and analysis that prepared the ground for the seed of inspiration to be planted in the minds of those of us in leadership in the two churches. Yet that inspiration was the crucial factor: without the conviction that God's hand was upon us, and that he was calling us to this task, we would not have gone forward. How God chooses to give inspiration to us will vary considerably. What is vital is that we look for it and are alert to it in whatever form it may come.

Essential for the receiving of such inspiration from God is a willingness to obey him, rather than do what we want, or what would most satisfy the expectations of the church and community we serve. Obedience sounds as if it is the opposite of creative originality, yet for the Christian that is not so. Tom Smail, in his fine book *The Forgotten Father*, expresses the nature of creative obedience in describing the ministry of Jesus in these terms:

> Every action of Jesus originates, and is directed by and towards the person, purpose and glory of the Father. It is from first to last *obedient* action, not initiating or innovating, but rather discerning and following. This is not a limitation on its spontaneity and freedom, but rather the source of it, because it is always personal response within a relationship, and never external conformity to impersonal rule and regulation.

Balance

Over the years I have come to appreciate the importance of maintaining a creative tension between intuition, analysis, and inspiration. On the working model I described it is possible to detach any one of the three strands. However, the result is that the ring no longer stays in the centre – indeed it almost goes right out of the picture, as the diagram below illustrates. So it is with learning leadership from experience.

If we pay attention only to intuition and to inspiration, but fail to give attention to analysis, we are likely to lead others into ill-prepared ventures, and at worst into enthusiasms neither we, nor they, can sustain because no adequate foundation has been laid. This is a particularly easy trap to fall into, and those who

Lost vision when any one factor is missing

want us to stop and think are likely to be made to feel 'unspiritual'. It happens when we act as though to say 'God has told us' rules out all thinking, questioning and planning. That is an unbiblical view of faith.

The apostle Paul, writing about the exercise of the gift of prophecy in 1 Corinthians 14, expressly says that when someone prophesies others should 'weigh it'. In other words when someone says 'God has told me/us . . .' the command is to switch our critical faculties *on* not *off*. If it is of God it will stand up to such scrutiny: if it is not of God then the sooner it is demolished the better for all concerned.

Similarly, if we pay attention only to intuition and analysis, we will cut off other people from the sense of God's call which is the only sound basis for sacrifice. We are also quite likely to mislead people about the distinction between natural, God-given, intuition, and that special inspiration which is his word to his church in a particular setting. Confusion about guidance will follow in the wake of such an approach. Furthermore we will miss the primary calling of the church, which is to discover and do the will of God rather than to establish or maintain an institution. We may end by creating a community of believers who serve God, but do not truly know him.

The situation in which inspiration and analysis are focused on but intuition is ignored, is less frequent but still happens. It will again result in loss of effectiveness because one third of the power of the engine that God has given has been shut down. We will find that we discover significant answers much less frequently with our creativity closed down, and those that we do find will often lack humanity. They may well be organisational answers only. The result will be a church which holds to the truth in a hard and insensitive way and which operates without openness in relationships.

Where the balance of all three elements is lacking, we lose out doubly. As the working model demonstrates, if one element is missing, not only is the benefit of that part lost, but the creative tension between the other two is also lost. Our need, in every situation, is therefore to be able to hold the balance between each of these three factors.

Bob Mumford, in his book *Take Another Look at Guidance*, uses a graphic illustration which makes this point well. Evidently there are three navigational lights for ships attempting to enter the harbour at Venice. It is a notoriously difficult task because of the amount of silting that continues to take place. The way that ships steer a safe course is to position themselves where all three lights are lined up and appear as one, which indicates that the ship is heading through the deepest channel to the safety of the harbour.

So with the interplay between inspiration, intuition, and analysis. All three need to be brought into play for a fully matured and rounded leadership to operate. Unlike the harbour lights, however, their inter-relationship is a subtle mobile in which there is a great variety of ways of harmonising the different elements. Yet, in the final issue, because the church is the called-out community (the literal meaning of the Greek word *ecclesia*) it is right to say 'So there remains intuition, analysis and inspiration, but the greatest of these is inspiration.'

A Theology of Learning from Experience
The discovery of God's agenda is surely the most crucial task of Christian leadership. In my experience, there is no more vital place to be discovering it than by willingly placing oneself on the anvil of experience in the place of vulnerability. This is my central thesis, that only in and through experience can truth

become incarnate – and that is God's purpose in calling men and women into leadership roles. The framework for learning which I have now developed is simply like the lights of Venice harbour. It enables me to chart my way through the experiences I have.

Having established this framework in this first part of the book, I am now almost ready to move on to the second part, in which I want to explore how these things have worked out in practice for me in the major areas of leadership I have been involved in.

However, there is one objection to all that I have said which I want to address before moving on, for the answer to it can better prepare the leader for the learning process I have been commending.

I want to deal with a question which arose in the early days of realising that I was on an anvil of God's design. The question was this: 'Is it not dangerous and unsound to allow our theology to arise out of, and be shaped by, experience?'

This was a pressing problem for me when I experienced a renewal in my relationship with God through the work of the Holy Spirit. I had been nurtured in charismatic horror stories of people who developed false theologies out of their experiences of the Spirit. I had been trained to avoid using historical books of the Bible, especially Acts, as the basis for any theological conclusions. Various insights gradually came together to help me in this quandary.

First, a little SCM theological monograph entitled *The God who acts*, written by Ernest Wright in 1948, had already prepared me in some measure for this time. I had picked it up while studying theology at Cambridge and had read it with interest. He was basically making the point that scripture sees the expression of truth through history-with-interpretation; hence the historical nature of much of scripture – not least the first five books of both the Old and New Testaments. Wright was raising fundamental questions about much so-called 'systematic theology' by asking why none of the biblical authors had been led to express truth in that distilled, rational way.

It was at this time that Francis Schaeffer was first making an impact on the evangelical world with his critique of what had happened to Christian thinking since the Enlightenment.

Together these two writers cautioned me that the over-cerebral form of the gospel expressed by much western Christianity was the product not of the biblical witness but of western rationalism.

However, it was on re-reading the Acts of the Apostles, after my experience of the Spirit, that I saw the apostles as supreme examples of men learning theology out of their experience. It was Peter on the roof-top at Joppa who first introduced me to what had happened. Here he was, with no scripture or other study material in his hand and no tutor to guide him, doing some of the most profound theology of all time ('then to Gentiles also is the gospel come'). His aid was nothing more rational than a pre-dinner nap and a fanciful dream. It was out of that that he became involved with Cornelius and later the whole Gentile world. Here was theology arising out of experience!

Once I had seen this, I was ready to see the whole of the apostles' teaching (especially as enshrined in the creeds of the church) in this light. They did not first sit down and work out the doctrine of the Trinity, the atonement, the incarnation, or Christology (their understanding of the person and work of Christ), and then seek to experience those truths. No, rather, they so experienced Jesus Christ that they finally came to the conclusion that he was in truth God in human form: and their experience of the Holy Spirit led them to the same conviction that he was part of, yet a distinct person within, the Godhead.

I am not arguing that all theology can be simply developed out of our experience of God. The evils of spiritualism, for example, arise out of an undifferentiated working back from experience. What I am speaking of however, is our need for a living dialogue between scripture and our experience, or at least our present understanding of scripture and our present experience of God. I have found myself slow to allow either my understanding of scripture or my present experience of God to be challenged: yet when this has happened I have so often found that it has been the next step in my own following after Jesus through which I have become better able to lead others. God-given intuition, analysis and inspiration, taken together, have enabled me to do this, and thereby to enter a little further into that continual learning experience which is at the heart of all true discipleship.

PART TWO

Practising the art

Chapter Five

DISCOVERING VISION

In Part One I have sought to establish a theology of learning from experience. At the heart of this has been the conviction that God is in the business of incarnating the truth in all believers, but especially in leaders of his church. I then went on to develop a framework for learning: the means by which we can interpret our experience and steer our way through many shoals that could bring disaster upon the leader and those who are being led.

In Part Two I want to go on to show how this learning process, and the framework that has been explained, have worked out in my experience. In doing so I have two aims in mind. I want to show that the theory does actually work in practice. This should not be too difficult since it was the theory which arose out of the experience, rather than the other way round. I also want to move on to highlight the major elements of leadership, and to share some of the lessons I have learned along the way.

This second part of the book is itself divided into two groups of chapters. In the first part the focus is on how to discover a vision with which to lead others, and how to move through to a place where that vision becomes reality. It would be good to see the church and its future as a blank sheet on which God wishes to write his purposes. However, the fact is that we all start with a less than perfect personality and a less than ideal church. This is why the final group of chapters addresses the practical and personal problems we are likely to find along the way. If these problems are not faced and overcome, they will for ever frustrate the implementation of vision: which is where true leadership begins – with an understanding of where we are going.

Ideas

Ideas hold communities together. They are the glue of groups, and the mortar of movements. In recent years we have seen the power of ideas on a global scale. Both the great superpowers have been defeated on the battlefield by small nations. America had to pull out of Vietnam, and Russia had to withdraw from Afghanistan, largely because the bonding force of ideas had held those peoples together against vastly superior fire power.

What is true for communities and nations is also evidenced in organisations such as multi-national businesses. Sir John Harvey-Jones, in *Making it Happen*, writes: 'The business that is not being purposefully led in a clear direction which is understood by its people is not going to survive, and all of history shows that is the case.'

For the church, too, we know from scripture and experience that 'where there is no vision the people perish' (Prov 29.18). Fighting for vision, including the battle to make time and stand back sufficiently to discover the call of God for the whole church, has been central to my experience of leadership.

Finding Direction

My intuitive determination to find direction for the church as well as for my own ministry, has been reinforced by several different analytical studies which underlined the importance of vision and direction and purpose in life.

One such study is the different ways in which the Greek and Hebrew cultures view history. The Greek way of seeing history is cyclical. It sees history as endlessly repeating itself in the same way that the rhythm of the seasons is repeated. By contrast the Hebraic view of history is linear: it expresses the idea of movement and direction given to human history by God. It is typified in the scriptures by the concept of a pilgrim people: Abraham going from Ur to the land of Canaan; Moses leading the children of Israel across the wilderness with a cloud by day and the pillar of fire by night to give them direction. The difference between these two approaches can be expressed diagrammatically:

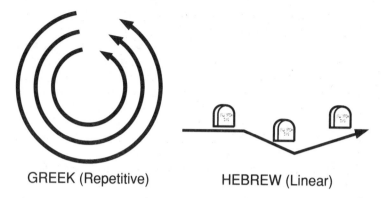

GREEK (Repetitive)   HEBREW (Linear)

The Greek and Hebrew view of history

The church is often trapped in the Greek view of the 'ceaseless round' of the church's year. So trapped that it sometimes does not even glimpse the need to discover the will of God for the particular situation it faces. I am not arguing for the abolition of all routines and festivals. Far from it, for modern man has lost much of the natural rhythm that God has built into creation (such as the sabbath rest), as well as much of the experience of holy days. However, our need is to move out beyond those patterns into an eagerness to discover and do the will of God.

A memorable example of this occurred early in my time at St Thomas's, when it became clear to me that the annual garden party was a massive investment of time, energy and manpower, for surprisingly little fruit. Most people in the church concentrated their efforts into it over a period of more than three months. Yet the money raised – a few hundred pounds – could have been multiplied many times over if we had simply held a gift day. The real reason for holding such an event actually had much more to do with the enjoyable experience we all had of working together on something. But was it not possible to 'work together' on making Christ known and forwarding the work of his kingdom? We dared to ask the question, and to stop the garden party. In this way we were able to break out of the ceaseless round and devote our energies to whatever God had for us as his next step. While I am not arguing for the abolition of all garden parties, it demonstrated to me how a costly pruning of our programme was to be part of our discipleship as a church.

The church which truly desires to reflect Christ to the world needs to be shaped by the same eagerness which he exhibited in his hunger to be about his Father's business. That is true whatever size operation we are involved in; whether it is a whole church, or a home group, a finance team, or a group of people leading worship or working with children. The goal is the will of God. It is that which should be our vision not the maintenance of annual traditions, however cherished they may be.

Another study on the importance of vision was about seeing the church as a pilgrim people. The idea of pilgrimage expresses, in vivid picture language, the Hebraic view of history, and it was this understanding of the church which came to me from an unexpected source during my early years in the ordained ministry. As part of post-ordination training I was required to read all the documents of the Vatican II Council. Protestantism being deeply embedded in me, I approached the text with reluctance and some hostility. Yet one of the abiding, and formative, effects of that studying was the notion of the church expressed in the words: 'Christ summons the Church, as she goes her pilgrim way, to that continual reformation of which she always has need.' That spoke to my sense of purpose and to my reading of the Scriptures. One particular passage became a map for me and spoke of the vision for the church that remains with me to this day. It reads:

> Coming forth from the eternal Father's love, founded in time by Christ the Redeemer, and made one in the Holy Spirit, the Church has a saving and an eschatological purpose which can be fully attained only in the future world. But she is already present in this world, and is composed of men, that is, members of the earthly city who have a call to form the family of God's children during the present history of the human race, and to keep increasing it until the Lord returns.
>
> This she does most of all by her healing and elevating impact on the dignity of the person, by the way in which she strengthens the seams of human society and imbues the everyday activities of men with a deeper meaning and importance. Thus, through her individual members and her whole community, the Church believes she can contribute greatly toward making the family of man and its history more human.

As a result of seeing the church in this way, I have found great help in looking back and seeing the various milestones, or stepping stones, along the way. I saw this so clearly as I looked back at the end of our building project and considered the journey of the church during the 1970s. First, there had been charismatic renewal which had brought faith to life. Then had come the development of the supporting fellowships which had transformed our openness and unity as a community of believers. Then had come the massive task of the building project. These major steps were all part of a superb plan with a marvellous strategy and progression built into them as they followed each other. That strategy and progression were not of my doing. I did not even notice them until I looked back, but they now enable me to discover vision.

During the time in which I was writing this book, we recognised our need as a church for fresh vision. In seeing God's way for the future, it was a great help to analyse the many steps we had taken, and to see where we were on our pilgrimage. Paradoxically we discerned that the first step was simply to stop. We had been involved in a series of major developments and were being called to a time of consolidation. Like the children of Israel entering the promised land under Joshua, our calling in this period was to 'get your supplies ready' (Jos 1.11). The cloud and pillar of fire would move, so the first need was to be refreshed and fully equipped for that next stage of the journey.

A variety of other studies to do with the value of goal setting, have added to my understanding of the need for vision. The first of these occurred when I attended an Evangelical Alliance management course in the late sixties run by an American Baptist minister, Olan Hendrix. He was an attractive and entertaining speaker who imparted much wisdom. A number of his quotations remain with me to this day as stars to steer by. Two in particular have stayed with me over the years. The first was: 'Most men don't plan to fail, they just fail to plan.' The second was: 'No group can be healthy unless it has a task outside of itself to fulfil.'

The coming together of these different studies has been a considerable aid to discovering vision afresh. We have realised that this truth applies to each of our four congregations. Each needs to be able to define its vision. Our first step into renewed vision has, therefore, been to get each of the four congregations to identify and give sharp focus to the specific mission it discerns as God's calling. It involves identifying the 'target group'. *Analysis* of how groups work told us that each congregation needs such a task. *Intuitively* we knew that the earlier loss of vision had to do with people feeling passengers in something run by others, rather than participants in something that belonged to them. At the *inspirational* level, we have found the stepping stones which are identified at the beginning of the book of Acts to be a framework for our own vision. There we read that Jesus said:

> 'You will receive power when the Holy Spirit comes on you; and you will be my witnesses in Jerusalem, and in all Judea and Samaria, and to the ends of the earth.'
>
> (Acts 1.8)

The picture is of concentric circles of the church's mission. Traditionally evangelicals have tended to major on 'the ends of the earth' and miss out the intervening stages. We have recognised in a fresh way that being involved in God's mission is not primarily what other people do in other countries, but what God calls us to do in our place.

Every church, group or activity needs that clarity of vision for its health and survival. But the question then arises as to how we can discover the appropriate vision for the group or church we are responsible for leading.

Ways into Vision

A few years ago I was taken by a member of the congregation to watch Sheffield Wednesday playing at Hillsborough. Although I had often watched football matches on television I had not been to a match since leaving school. When the first goal was scored I suddenly felt incredibly bereft. There was no action replay! There was no chance to review what happened: the event had gone for ever. The opportunity to relive experiences has been an important means of learning. As I look back I can see four ways in which God's direction has repeatedly come.

First is the importance of knowing your calling. Stopping to reflect on God's leading has brought me back again and again to where I came in to both the Christian faith and the ordained ministry. The original call has not changed, it has just matured. When I step outside of that calling – which is summed up for me in one text, namely 'to equip the saints for the work of ministry' – I am aware that authority and effectiveness depart.

A very thorough statistical survey of the church was done in 1978. One interesting, and humbling, fact was that only four per cent of those who had come to faith had done so as a result of the preaching, yet over sixty per cent had been brought to faith through the friendship of a member of the church. It was particularly striking to those who had done the analysis because they had just come from a church where sixty per cent of the members had been won to faith by the preaching of the vicar.

David Wasdell, who had conducted the survey, considered that St Thomas's was in a more healthy state. He then propounded his theory of church growth leadership based on these facts, namely that the ideal leader is one who has no gifts at all! However he did admit to the fact that such a leader would need one gift – the ability to mobilise the gifts of the whole membership. I know that has been my primary calling.

Another element in my own call has been the conviction that God intends the church to grow, not because he has any special delight in big churches, but because his desire is that all should come to faith. If that is to happen the church must find ways in which to keep its doors open. There needs not only to be a seat to sit on, but also room in the fellowship, room for service, and room simply to belong. That conviction has returned again and again to disturb me just at the point at which I or the church had been about to settle down into a cosy club mentality.

Catherine Marshall, in her book *Beyond Ourselves*, writes about the importance of 'dreaming dreams'. What she says in this chapter is that each of us needs to get in touch with what our calling from God truly is. I am convinced that each one of us has such a call – not just those in the ordained ministry, or the caring professions. Every believer has a unique call from God. We need to stay true to it and learn to operate from within it.

As I have looked at the life of Jesus I have seen how he lived out of a sense of call from God. His desire to discover and do the

75

Father's will was the inspiration for the whole of his living. To the tempter he said:

> 'It is written: "Man does not live by bread alone, but on every word that comes from the mouth of God".'
>
> (Matt 4.4)

To the disciples who had just gone to fetch a meal at the end of a long day of walking, he said:

> 'I have food to eat that you know nothing about . . . My food . . . is to do the will of him who sent me and to finish his work.'
>
> (Jn 4.3, 4)

Moreover he had a very special and sacred use for a word which we use much too frequently in the church: 'must'. We use it to describe a multitude of things that we want, or feel under obligation to give others. Jesus used it only and always to describe the known will of God for him. 'I must be in my Father's house', 'I must preach to the other villages also', 'I must go up to Jerusalem', and finally 'the Son of man must suffer many things.'

This inner directedness was the secret of his strength in handling the pressure of other people's expectations. Such obedience to the Father involved Jesus in making costly choices. He was not to be found doing things that pleased others – even his disciples. The same holy ruthlessness needs to be the characteristic of the church if it is to function effectively. We need to know that unique calling of God to each of us and to discover the vision God wants to give us in that context.

Second is the importance of watching the Father. One verse from John's Gospel became a vital guide in this.

> 'The Son does nothing of his own accord, but only what he sees the Father doing.'
>
> (Jn 5.19)

It was in the early 1970s that those of us on the staff team began to ask ourselves what we saw the Father doing. When we did so we saw God bringing people together in small groups and helping them to be open to him and to each other. It was out of this reflection that we later established the fellowship groups which have been a vital part of the health and growth of the church.

Years later, when we asked the question again we saw how many people, both as individuals, and in groups, were moving out into the community and city around us. Out of this we developed the logo for our monthly newsheet to remind us all of what God was calling us to do. It has proved very helpful for us to 'write the vision so that he who runs may read' as Habakkuk puts it (Hab 2.2, RSV). Our current vision reads:

> ST THOMAS'S, CROOKES
> *moving out*
> *in boldness*
> *power and*
> *the love of God.*

Learning to 'see' what the Father is doing has taken time. It needs the gift of discernment, which is the ability to distinguish between spirits; that is, the ability to tell whether something is motivated by God, the flesh, or the devil. Intuition has played an important part in this form of 'seeing'. It is vital, if someone comes, even when they are saying 'God has told me . . .', for us to know whether we need to help them come to terms with some immature part in their make-up, or whether this is of God and requires our full and immediate co-operation. Often there is a mixture of flesh and spirit. The gift of discernment includes, therefore, the ability to separate the truth content while discarding the wrapping. There needs to be a distinguishing between the two if we are to be able to discern the vision which is revealed as we watch for the working of the Father.

Third is the importance of listening to the Spirit. It has been a journey itself learning how to do just that. I have already written about prophetic words, and learning to listen to the church, and learning through problems. But a question arises as to how we know it is the Spirit, and how we can distinguish his voice from our own hopes and fears.

Gethsemane has been crucial in my learning this. In his prayer in the garden, Jesus first owned his own emotions ('Father, if it is possible, let this cup pass from me'), before going on to surrender himself freely to the will of the Father ('nevertheless not my will but yours be done'). Owning up to how I feel about a situation has been very important in discovering God's will. Sometimes he does act in the direction of my hopes, at other times my worst fears are realised. Often his way involves fulfilling the hopes through facing the fears.

What has been important has been learning to combine honesty with faith. Honesty without faith can lead to despair. Faith without honesty can result in pretence. Sir John Harvey-Jones says, 'The greatest help in setting a strategy is a hefty slice of cynicism and the openness of mind to re-examine cherished beliefs.' Often we are faced with imperfect situations in which we do not have all the facts and yet a decision needs to be made. I seek to go for the answer which holds the most integrity and which I am prepared to live with even if I am proved to be wrong.

Recently we experienced a significant shortfall in giving. As we faced the problem we sought to *analyse* what was going on and had some people working on the statistics of giving to see if they could discern trends. We also listened to our *intuition*, sensing that there were problems but no great crisis in the church (as there had been in similar circumstances before).

We also sought to listen to the church. We did this by my writing a letter to every member explaining the financial situation and then saying that such problems often indicate a spiritual malaise. People were invited to comment on what they thought was wrong. One or two people took the opportunity to berate the church about their pet hobby horses, but most gave a considered and prayerful response. As a result we have done a number of things, not least to declare the next twelve months, a time of consolidation in which to work on the problems the church had identified. The picture of the children of Israel not only following the cloud by day and pillar of fire by night, but also learning to stop when the cloud and fire stopped have been an important *inspiration* for us in this step.

Fourth is the vital role of studying the scriptures in the discovery of vision. It was the word of God which was the coal face from which Jesus mined his understanding of the Father's will. Indeed, I have long pondered on just how he did that. When you look at some of the central themes of his teaching, God's word is clearly the creative force. Yet one is left asking just how did Jesus see that the heart of the biblical message was love, or where did his understanding of the kingdom find roots in the Old Testament, and how did he see that the Messiah must suffer? The answer I have come to is that, like his mother, Jesus 'pondered all these things in his heart'. Meditating on the scriptures he heard them at their deepest level. No wonder he urged his disciples to listen: 'he who has ears to hear, let him hear'. Our experience of renewal has been one of God continually removing the brackets that our unbelief has put around much of God's word.

When renewal first emerged we went back to the scriptures as a church to see what they said. I wrote a thirty-five page study booklet to help the church as we sought to establish if this was truly of God. The example of the Bereans is a great inspiration in this process:

> Now the Bereans were of more noble character than the Thessalonians, for they received the message with great eagerness and examined the Scriptures every day to see if what Paul said was true.
>
> (Acts 17.11)

When a number of years later, we were introduced by John Wimber, to the Signs and Wonders dimension of the kingdom, we again set up times for the church to study God's word. 'Kingdom workshops' we called them, in which we both taught and practised these things. We deliberately held these after the Sunday evening service. No one had anything forced on them. Rather we were able to explore these new insights in a setting that minimised the sense of threat: though the way the Holy Spirit worked was disturbing enough for us all!

Too Many Good Ideas

Much of what I have said so far could be understood as directed to those who find it difficult to discover vision, and who tend to have little in the way of creative ideas. However, for some of us – among whom I number myself – the problem is not lack of ideas, but too many. Our tendency is to exhaust ourselves and our churches with all the ideas we feel urged to pursue. The problem then becomes, not what idea shall we follow, but which of the hundred possibilities really contains the call of God?

I was so aware of this at one stage in the life of St Thomas's that I said, 'What we need here is an ideas contraceptive!' Our problem was that so many ideas were being conceived that we were faced either with the painful process of aborting them, or with the impossible task of keeping them all alive once they came to term. Too many became stillborn.

I could not see, however, anything in scripture which corresponded to an ideas contraceptive. What I did see, though, was men like David and Moses 'enquiring of the Lord' about what they did, and Jesus waiting for the divine 'must' to direct his actions. Seeing this turned my thinking on its head. It was not an ideas contraceptive we needed, but rather the bringing of all our ideas before God in prayer, for him to cause just one, or occasionally two, to be brought to life. Our task was to wait on God, with our ideas, for the fertilising power of the Holy Spirit to come upon the one which was part of his plan for us.

There is one very striking incident of David 'enquiring of the Lord'. He and his men came home after battle and 'found it destroyed by fire and their wives and sons and daughters taken captive' (1 Sam 30.3). Included in the list of captives are both David's wives. He and his army are devastated and give themselves over to loud weeping. Then they have to decide what to do. Everything in them, their reason and their feelings must surely have shouted out for action, revenge and pursuit. Yet, amazingly David's response is to send for the priest and the ephod and to enquire of the Lord, 'Shall I pursue this raiding party?' (1 Sam 30.7). In this way David allows inspiration to take control over analysis and intuition.

I have found this a hard but vital discipline, to bring even the most cogent and moving reasons for action, before God in prayer for him to direct our actions. Yet it has been a healthy and essential way of handling a highly creative congregation and leadership team; only moving when the Spirit so directs. It saves much effort and a great deal of frustration, and leads us more quickly into the vision God has for us.

A Changing Mobile
The discovery of a robust and authentic vision comes about when inspiration, intuition, and analysis are all functioning together to hold us in the centre of God's will for his church. Yet how these three inter-relate has been different in each experience. They are a living trinity of factors which, like a mobile, are always changing their position and their relationship to each other.

In the building project vision came wave upon wave on an incoming tide. Advance was made all the time, but not without a constant process of undertow away from the overall direction, and a repeated sense of having things taken from us. The first wave was one of *analysis*. We became increasingly aware of how inappropriate, inefficient, and frustrating our buildings were to our emerging vision of church life. Our solutions, in retrospect, were very puny. They were about moving some pews here, and putting up a Portakabin there, and were in another league from the scale of God's purposes we eventually found ourselves being led into.

The second wave came in a moment of *intuition* at the vicarage when the wardens and I met to hear details of an offer to buy the land on which our out-of-the-way church hall stood. Out of our response came the seed idea of moving all our buildings onto one site. At the time we used three buildings: the church, the nearby school, and the remote church hall. Again our solutions were timid compared with the strength of the answers that eventually emerged. We thought of moving our prefabricated hall onto the churchyard. But the notion of *one* building had been conceived. The rest was merely the outworking of that one seminal idea.

The third wave was a growing sense of call, a conviction that God's *inspiration* lay behind our thinking. This took months and even years and probably never washed over some people at all. However, the tide was strong enough to catch up the vast majority of the church and to move us to places where we had never dreamt of being.

Other ventures emerged out of a very different mixture.

The establishing of fellowship groups arose out of a direct word of prophecy (inspiration). It took us eighteen months to grasp the significance of this word from God. That understanding of what God was saying was the result of a series of intuitive insights. Analysis of the situation, and of how groups work, came right at the end.

The local ecumenical project began with an *intuitive* thought about the Baptist church 'coming back with us' when we returned from using their building while our church was being rebuilt. Only after a sense of God's *inspiration* being behind the possibility, did we begin to do detailed *analysis* about the feasibility and nature of such a united venture.

The establishing of the nine o'clock service happened as a result of a direct word of *inspiration* to me that God wanted to add 'one or two hundred' young people to the church within a matter of months. It was followed – within the week – by an *intuitive* response that this could only happen if the young people within the church were given freedom to develop an appropriate form of worship themselves. Then began the detailed work of *analysis* of how best to do it. Indeed, some did – and still do – say that insufficient time was given to iron out the many issues that needed to be faced before we started. As evidence they would point to the many struggles we had, subsequent to the launch, to achieve an integration of the nine o'clock service with the whole church. They could well have been right. My judgement was that inspiration, intuition, and analysis were all sufficiently lined up and woven together to make it the right time for action. Like the farmer, faced with a knife-edge decision about whether to wait one more day for the ripening of the harvest or to act now before the rains come, the Christian leader constantly faces difficult decisions about timing. Waiting too long means that the opportunity has gone: premature action can lead to the stillbirth of genuine vision.

Pondering These Things
All that I have said about discovering vision presupposes and requires one particular practice above all else. We need to listen – deeply. I would identify the quality of listening as the key to effectiveness in the discovery of vision. Vital to such listening is an openness to two special elements in God's ways. First is the largeness of vision he has. Even our greatest dreams are insipid compared to the rich wine of his purposes. Again and again I have had to be stretched to take in the greatness and depth of God's plans.

Second is the fact that what God desires to do seems always beyond our predicting. I often look back at my time so far at St Thomas's and realise that no group of people could ever have sat down and said 'Next year what we ought to do is . . . a two-thirds of a million pounds building project . . . form a united church with the Baptists . . . start a youth culture congregation . . .' and so on. Which is why being open to the scale of God's plans, and to his surprises is so vital. That openness comes about, above all, through exercising the faith to listen.

Morton Kelsey in his book *The Other Side of Silence* illustrates this quality of listening so well in what he says about Martin Luther King:

> One reason for the power of the social action of Martin Luther King was the way it sprang out of his wholeness which was the wholeness of a person recollected in silence and the presence of God. Almost all Christian reform of any significance which in the end healed rather than destroyed, has sprung out of the same source. Silence can be a mini-experience of death and resurrection. It is a temporary cessation of one's doing and planning and desires. When we actually die, we give up the possessions that have mattered to us and entrust them to the care of others. Much the same thing happens when one stops in silence. Action, planning, desiring are all suspended, entrusted to the Other in silence, while the thoughts and emotions and realities that surround them are given a chance to regroup.

One of the most vital things, therefore, that we can offer to God on the anvil of experience is our openness to him and his purposes, and an expectancy that there is always new vision he desires to give us. That listening is a vital element of our availability as malleable metal on which he is working.

It is right that we work hard to plan and organise and set goals. God seems pleased to work in such an environment. Yet he remains Lord of the church and the agenda is ultimately his. Our experience has been that all the major developments in the life of the church have essentially been his surprises. The most important thing that we have had to offer has been a willingness to listen, to reflect, and – at the right time – to act on what he has been saying. There seems to be a direct correlation between the quality of our listening, and God's readiness to act.

Chapter Six

TRANSFERRING VISION

It is never an easy task to take people with you into vision – but it is almost impossible to do so if you do not know where you are going! Indeed, as the writer of Proverbs puts it: 'Where there is no vision the people perish' (Prov 29.18). The importance of knowing the call of God is central throughout scripture. It was in response to this that Abraham left the security of his homeland and set out for an unknown destination. It was because of what God said to Moses at the burning bush, to David through the anointing by Samuel, and to Isaiah in the Temple, that these men had the courage to act and take others with them.

The same pattern is evident in the New Testament. Jesus is the supreme example of a man knowing the call of God. For that reason his call to the disciples to follow him was central to his relationship with them. The Acts of the Apostles is the story of a church moving in response to the repeated call of God – not least the call to do the strange and novel and inexplicable.

It is the call of God alone which is able to guide and sustain the church. Yet for this to happen, that call of God has to be both received and owned not just by the overall leaders but by the church or group as a whole.

Transferring the vision, whether it is for a major building programme, or for the development of a home group of ten people, needs to be done equally well, and it is the responsibility of the leader to learn how to do it thoroughly and effectively.

Three crucial aspects of this process of transferring vision stand out from my experience. First is the importance of the whole church discovering vision together in *prayer*. Second is the vital part that a two-way *dialogue* between the leaders and members of any group plays in that transfer of conviction. Third is the powerful effect of *delegation* in enabling others to 'buy into the vision' of a group. In this chapter I want to look at these factors, each of which is so different from the others yet essential if vision is to be transferred properly. I also want to uncover how inspiration, intuition and analysis have been interwoven in my own experience of seeking to incorporate all three factors in the process of passing on vision to the whole church.

The Power of Prayer

A study of the Gospels and the Acts of the Apostles reveals how, for both Jesus and the early church, all the major steps in their different callings were the fruit of direct and specific prayer. It has been in prayer that most of our major steps forward as a church have not only been conceived but also grasped by the whole membership. I was fortunate in working under Michael Baughen as my first vicar for he held firmly to the conviction that praying together had to be at the heart of the life of a church. Moving to Wolverhampton, I discovered from experience that my intuition to set up a monthly, and then weekly, prayer meeting proved to be the means of the church catching fire in the spiritual realm. People began to 'see' what the preaching had been about, and what their part in the life of the church should be.

Arriving in Crookes I discovered that I had inherited a weekly prayer meeting which was attended by about twenty people. It was not only the praying heart of the church, it *was* the heart of the church. This is where God spoke, and was experienced, and where the core of the membership was cemented together in love. Our experience of renewal, the major changes in the whole worship style of the church, the development of fellowship groups, and the launching of the building project were all brought to birth in this meeting. But not only did such major developments begin in those prayer meetings, it was there that vision was grasped by the great majority of those who came. They heard and received the call of God to his church.

Inspiration broke through and moved the heart of the membership of the church through our unitedly waiting on God in prayer.

However, one of the strange effects of charismatic renewal on St Thomas's has been the demise of the mid-week prayer meeting. It has been replaced by home groups, as it has in many churches which would not wish to call themselves charismatic. Such groups have indeed proved fundamental to the growth of the church; yet there is something unhealthy about their replacing the united prayer. Significantly it was during the time of greatest spiritual dryness, and related leadership conflict, that we were not praying together as a whole church. We learned from experience – the hard way – that 'the church which prays together, stays together'.

Learning Corporate Prayer

Out of that experience we built praying together as a whole church back into our programme. We now hold a *central prayer meeting (CPM)* on the first Wednesday of every month, with the fellowship groups meeting on the remaining three or four Wednesdays of the month.

I frequently hear of churches that recognise the need to pray together, and have even tried to do so, but have never seen the prayer meeting becoming a vital part of the life of the church. Where an attempt is made to hold a monthly meeting church members seem to take it as a night off and only a handful come to pray. Part of the answer is to stay with that handful, and make that meeting so special that they act like light to moths and draw others in. To 'turn on the light' at such a meeting is, however, as great a test of a leader's walk with God, and love for others, as can be found.

Developing prayer at the heart of the church has involved us in ruthless and thorough-going analysis of the reasons for poor attendances. For much of the time the result of that analysis has led us to change how we run the meeting. Occasionally it has involved challenging the church about its commitment to corporate prayer. Fascinatingly it has been *analysis* and *intuition* which have enabled us to develop a monthly prayer meeting which is devoted to discovering God's *inspiration* for his church.

In addition to the normal problems of motivating a church to pray together we have also had some major additional and local complications. It has not been easy to find a way of integrating the worship and prayer style of two distinct cultural groups represented by the main body of the church on the one hand, and the urban youth culture of the nine o'clock service on the other. We have not achieved it fully yet, indeed we are still grappling with the complexity of running a prayer meeting with an attendance of over three hundred. Yet what we have found is I believe of relevance to a prayer meeting of almost any size, worship style or form of intercession.

Three particular things have proved to be important. First, it needs to be a good *information time* when the church is told about what is actually going on, what the problems are and what the plans are. If you want to know what is happening at St Thomas's then come to the CPM. Second, we have found that it needs to be a *vision time* when the purpose of all that we are doing and the direction in which we are heading are given high profile. Third, we have discovered that the best way to ensure that it is well attended is to put plenty of resources into the event so that it is a *quality time*. Our goal is simply for it to be the best meeting of the month – even though the goal-posts often seem to be moving.

Analysis of Prayer

The CPM is usually divided into two parts. One is devoted to a whole church mode in which we are together in one group and spend time in worship, brief reports (no more than two an evening, rarely more than five minutes long), a pastoral address (dealing with some aspect of the overall vision) and rooted in scripture, followed by time for prayer.

The other half we spend in the four congregational groups (with between thirty and one hundred and thirty people in each group). Here we share congregational concerns and spend a higher proportion of time in prayer about specific issues.

By analysing our experience of corporate prayer we have identified five different styles of corporate prayer, although we practise only three of them on a frequent basis. We have identified them by their sources of origin, to us, and rated them according to how far they aid participation, and how far they aid unity in the sense of the whole church praying together. Those five styles are identified in the table below.

Prayer type (our names)	form	aid to participation	aid to unity
Yonggi Cho	everyone praying aloud at the same time	* * * * *	* *
Wimber	praying in small groups of three to eight	* * * *	* *
Keswick	one person at a time praying aloud	* * *	* * * * *
Cathedral	led intercessions by a 'minister'	* *	* * * *
Taizé	complete silence	*	* * *

It is dangerous to rate each style in terms of its aid to participation and unity since each style can be done well or badly and is likely to cover quite a range. However the scores approximate to our normal experience of how each works. Two in particular need comment on.

First, we are most familiar with the traditional evangelical style, which we call the 'Keswick' model. We are also most familiar with its limitations. The bigger the group, the less people feel able to participate, and the bigger the temptation to pray what I call 'horizontal' prayers ('Lord renew in the staff a love for . . .', or 'We ask your blessing/judgement on the meeting about the ordination of women being held at 2.30 p.m. on Tuesday week in the church hall . . .'!). It is also liable to the dangers of hidden liturgy: the same small number of people praying the same, set, prayers month after month. They remind me of the story of the man who in some weekly prayer meeting prayed every week for thirteen years 'Lord, remove the cobwebs from the eyes of those who do not believe.' Eventually someone was sufficiently exasperated to shout out after the repetition of that prayer one week 'Lord, kill the spider!' We have found the 'Keswick' model more effective in the smaller congregational groupings.

We have tried a few changes in the 'rules of engagement' which have helped to overcome some of the problems; for example we have asked people to put up their hand if they wish to pray, and then to stand to aid audibility. This gives the leader the opportunity to give space between prayers, and to give those who pray less frequently (and are often therefore more likely to be moved of the Spirit to pray on this occasion) the 'air space' they need.

Second, is the 'Yonggi Cho' method. It is based on the Pentecostal understanding of Acts 4.24 ('When they heard this, they raised their voices together in prayer to God'), its name coming from the name of the pastor of the world's largest church (in Seoul, South Korea) who has developed this pattern of prayer as a major characteristic of his church. It is the least natural to our reserved English temperament, yet we have found it to be a method that, probably more than any other, produces a strong sense of the presence of God. We had to break through the embarrassment barrier and the feeling of artificiality. For this reason we practised for several consecutive months until we felt comfortable with this pattern.

We lead into this form of prayer through worship. At the end of the last song the worship team improvise on their instruments as a musical backing to the prayer, providing an aid to such prayer in just the same way that an organ is an aid to singing by filling the space between the voices. Someone at the front introduces specific topics every few minutes. The topics have usually been introduced before the time of worship began so that people would know what is coming. The topics are progressively uncovered on the overhead projector as we pray; this avoids the need for people to have to try and remember what we are meant to be praying about.

The primary experience of this type of prayer is one of being stretched in prayer and of having prayers 'drawn out of oneself', often to our own surprise. It is stretching to pray for the children's work, or our witness at work, or to praise God for the Cross, in an unprepared but spoken prayer of two or three minutes. Indeed it can feel like holy aerobics, in which spiritual muscles are stretched and toned up.

Our present practice is to concentrate on these two types, together with breaking into small groups of about half a dozen people to pray. We use just one or two of these models at any one meeting. However, our goal is to broaden the range of worship and prayer styles. Long-term we may well develop other styles: and even discover new ways as well.

It is important to point out that although a prayer meeting is about discovering God's *inspiration*, we have only been able to develop the CPM as far as we have by listening to the whole church's *intuition*, and by very thorough *analysis* of the details of each method of praying together. Ultimately, though, it is not the style of prayer which matters; it is the fact that if we are to be united as a church in vision, we must be united in joining in prayer concerning that vision. Only in this way can we receive as one body the vision God desires to transfer to the church as a whole.

Vision Building Together

Prayer is about both talking to and listening to God. Second only to this vital dialogue, in the matter of transferring vision, is the importance of real dialogue between leaders and members of any group, in which there need to be three strands.

The first strand of such effective dialogue involves the courage to give a clear lead. The pulpit ministry is the single most important element in this.

For example, when charismatic renewal had an impact on my life, I devoted much time to studying the scriptures, re-reading them in the light of my experience. The teaching that resulted won over a good number who felt that what was happening was 'unbiblical', and we discovered together the difference between something being 'unbiblical' and 'unfamiliar'. By giving a biblical base, it therefore gave a proper control to a movement which could otherwise have had experience as its only test of validity. It also enabled me to establish some ground rules – such as learning to respect each other when our thinking or theology was different. Out of this emerged an important healing and maturing process which was to bear fruit in later years as well. When, twelve years later, we became involved in the 'signs and wonders' ministry we again began to communicate the vision to the church through teaching, both at Sunday services and at special events. The same pattern of response resulted. Similarly, when the church had to make decisions together about establishing the local ecumenical project, the giving of a clear lead from both the Anglican and Baptist pulpits was of great importance.

In giving a clear lead one is giving inspiration to others. This happens, for us, through such means as writing in the monthly magazine, speaking at the central prayer meeting, in personal conversations, and even through the giving of the notices in services!

The importance of this exercise of leadership came home to me particularly as we moved on from the building project to consider whether God was calling us to unite with Crookes Baptist church. We called a meeting and set the issues before the church in as objective a way as was possible. I was wanting the church to make up its own mind. Yet at that meeting a number of people were saying, in different ways, 'You are the leader, you tell us.' They were expecting me to give the lead: a democratic majority was not going to convince the church that this was the will of God. It forced me back to prayer and waiting for God to give me the conviction that this was the road he wanted me to go down. I was hesitant because I had realised, during the building project, what disaster would follow if I had been leading the church on a path that was not of God's choosing. When I was able to communicate my conviction that this was God's call to us, the church was then able to examine the idea and consider adopting it. I was learning the truth of what President Eisenhower once said about leading others. He commented that getting a group of people to move position is like making a piece of string move. If you push it, very little movement takes place – other than the creation of a tangle. Pulling from the front, however, causes the whole of the rest of the string to follow.

Although this 'up front' leadership is vital, I am convinced that it needs to be seen as a passing phase and as an instrument of the higher goal of transferring the vision to the whole church. Experience has taught me that 'up front', charismatic leadership (in the 'follow me, I know the way' sense), is often necessary to move a group of people from one place or attitude to another. However, it is not the way to sustain people in a commitment to that vision. For the long haul the vision needs to be transferred to the whole membership. The people of Samaria illustrated this in response to the 'leadership' of the woman at the well when they said to her 'We no longer believe just because of what you said; now we have heard for ourselves, and we know that this man really is the Saviour of the world' (Jn 4.42).

When we discerned that moving into 'congregations' was the right path, we took time to share that possibility with the whole church. One of the ways that we did this was to call the leaders of our fellowship groups together to explain what we meant and why we believed it was of God. We then sent them back to their groups to talk it over before reporting back.

During the course of that reporting back one of the most traditional group leaders, who had opposed all changes in the church up to this point, said – with considerable exasperation 'Why don't we get on and do this, rather than wasting all our time talking about it endlessly?' Jokingly I replied 'Don't rush me, I am getting old nowadays and I need time to adjust to new ideas!' However, the fact that someone most likely to be resistant to change was arguing for it made it evident to me that the time had come to act. The vision, which had begun with a clear 'up front' lead, had been transferred sufficiently for the change to be implemented. Had we gone ahead with our move into congregations before that consensus had been achieved, they would not have been the success they have proved to be.

Listening Leadership

Transferring the vision needs to take place not only in prayer, but also in a two-way dialogue between the leaders and members of a group, most obviously through the leaders speaking and communicating vision. However, there is another, and vital side to this dialogue.

The second strand of effective dialogue involves the willingness and ability to listen to the church. Sadly we leaders are not very good at this. We easily become threatened and feel we are being criticised when it is simply a matter of people arguing the issues through. Alternatively we can sit patiently while others 'have their say', yet inwardly are closed to any change in our thinking. 'My mind is made up, don't confuse me with the facts' is not an effective leadership style. Not to listen to and harness the gifts and insights of the whole church is both arrogance and folly.

'Listen to all the conversations of the world,' said Paul Tournier, 'they are for the most part the dialogues of the deaf.' How tragic yet how true – even in the church. Learning to listen is a difficult skill, but an essential task if the creativity, faith and insight of the whole body is to be harnessed. The result will often be that the wise leader learns to adopt the vision of the membership. By this I mean that it is not necessarily I or the leadership who have the vision. Leaders need to be able to hear and see God's vision when it comes through the members – or indeed even through unbelieving outsiders if that is how God chooses to speak. Moses showed his meekness in being open to the advice of his father-in-law, Jethro; and indeed much of the shape of our own church's service of the community has been the fruit of our having learned to do just this. The launching of the Harvest coffee shop, the initiation of mother and toddler groups, and more recently the starting of a monthly mid-week 'pram service' (called the Ark service), have all been developments that emerged out of the vision that members of the church had. Like two well-known recent bank slogans, we have learned to be the 'listening' church that 'likes to say yes' to such vision.

Should it be thought that this is difficult with one hundred or more members of a church, then reflect on the words of Sir John Harvey-Jones, in *Making it Happen*, about how he sought to develop such a dialogue in a company employing tens of thousands of people, of many nationalities and diverse skills, involved in a global operation.

> In deciding where we should go we have to transfer 'ownership' of the direction by involving everyone in the decision. Making it happen means involving the hearts and minds of those who have to execute and deliver . . . I advocated the creation of the vision of where the company should be going by means of an iterative process combining both bottom-up and top-down planning.

He then wisely adds:

> There is no way in which a vision of the future can be developed among a group of people unless those people have a very high

degree of mutuality of respect, tolerance, and above all humour
. . . plain speaking and tolerance are tender flowers which have to
be nurtured and helped to grow.

Taking Time

Giving clear leadership and learning to listen need an additional
element to make them work.

*The third strand of effective dialogue involves giving time and
space for the assimilation of new ideas.* This we have found to be
vital in order to let people discuss, argue about and indeed
disagree with ideas when they are shared. The need arises
because a leadership group may have to spend hours wrestling
with some problem before careful and prayerful consideration
enables it to see the way through and believe that God is in it. It
comes as a shock if the idea, when shared with the church, is
greeted with doubt and questioning. This will happen, however,
not necessarily because of the unbelief and rebelliousness of the
people of God but rather because they are only where the
leadership group was when it began to consider the matter.
There has not been enough space and time to assimilate the new
idea. The church may not be sure it sees the problem: no wonder it
struggles to grasp the solution with enthusiasm! Only by working the matter through are most people convinced about solutions
to problems. In a church led by a full-time staff team this problem of being ahead of the rest of the church has been a particular
danger. We have had to learn to give people time to catch up.

We now seek to share problems in leadership groups, and with
the whole church, as soon as they surface. I am keen to share
those difficulties well before we have begun to look for answers.
The whole membership has a vital role in clearly identifying the
problem.

People need to be able to look at the arguments and convince
themselves. Yet in a Christian context it is easy to feel guilty,
disloyal and rebellious in expressing a contrary opinion. As
leaders we need to have the confidence to let ideas out and allow
others to knock them about. What is of God will remain standing: indeed it will usually be matured and developed by such
argument.

Several quotations spring to my mind in situations like this and encourage me to go through this healthy conflict process of assimilation. Proverbs teaches that: 'As iron sharpens iron, so one man sharpens another' (Prov 27.17). The apostle Paul said: 'No doubt there have to be differences among you to show which of you have God's approval' (1 Cor 11.19). Sir John Harvey-Jones (in *Making it Happen*) quotes the comment of a wise manager who pointed out that 'in industry the optimum level of conflict is not zero'. He then goes on to say, 'A high degree of constructive conflict is almost essential in the process . . . if the right decisions are to be taken it is essential that conflicting views are heard and thrashed out.'

Sadly, in church circles two forces inhibit this process. False notions of submission make people feel guilty about disagreeing with the leaders. Also leaders feel threatened by anything less than unanimous acclaim for their ideas. I understand their feeling. A creative, God-given, idea does feel like 'our baby' and we naturally leap to its defence. Yet that course is counter-productive. It is our insecurity that is picked up and transferred rather than the vision. If the baby is to grow it must be allowed to make its own way in the world.

For vision to be grasped and worked through there needs to be free and willing agreement to it on behalf of the members. That will happen only when people have the time to talk, think and pray about the whole matter. It has been hard to learn this lesson, for when I get an idea I want to do it today. I have had to learn to be patient and wait. Sometimes that waiting has been for years, with no guarantee that the vision would ever be implemented. It has nonetheless been a crucial lesson to learn.

Leading, listening and allowing time for the process of assimilation have been the three vital strands in this dialogue. They have emerged as the result of *intuition*, together with learning from experience. These insights have often led on to a detailed *analysis* of some issue (perhaps raised by a member of the church), and out of this process God's *inspiration* of the whole church has been greatly enriched as well as transferred to many others.

Releasing Energy Through Delegation
We have seen how transferring the vision needs to happen at the

spiritual level through uniting in prayer, and at the level of dialogue as leaders both listen and give space. But it also needs to happen at the practical level. This is achieved sometimes most powerfully when other people are given permission to get on with doing a particular task, within an appropriate structure. Not only is the vision transferred in practice through such delegation, but great energy can also be released to extend the vision. This is the ultimate proof that the church has 'bought into' the vision.

I first saw the effect of such authority during the building project. The two churchwardens and I found ourselves shouldering a massive responsibility in seeing the whole venture through. We were often making decisions which would add tens of thousands of pounds to the costs. Obviously we kept the church council informed. For their part they had sufficient confidence in us to encourage us to continue with that authority. In fact I think they were more comfortable with that than we were! It certainly sharpened the vision which the three of us had.

This pattern is one we have repeated regularly with great effect. Giving authority to one or more individuals to head up our worship ministry, the children's work, the care of our buildings, the mother and toddlers work, the nine o'clock service and so on has greatly stimulated vision in each of those areas. My task has more often been one of catching up with the vision of others, rather than instilling vision. Much of the growth of the church in recent years has been the fruit of this willingness to let others tackle problems. Such delegation is far more than getting other people to implement my solutions, although I am not afraid to tell them what I think. It involves the risk of giving others the problem, and allowing them to come up with their unique solutions. I now describe delegation as 'the noble art of defining a problem for someone else to solve'. It involves allowing others space to look at the problem and come up with *their* solutions. It also involves giving them sufficient authority to get on and do the job.

I have learned to watch for *inspiration* in delegation, especially when seeking the right person to delegate a task to. Here I have discovered, the hard way, that mental laziness can hinder the work of God. When I see a job to be done, obvious names come to mind: they may be the right people, but more often than not

God seems to have someone else in mind. I now look for one particular hallmark – a person who has vision. Regardless of all other factors and giftedness, the person who lacks vision lacks the vital key. So, not always going straight away for the obvious person, but waiting on God in prayer for the person he anoints (just as Samuel was surprised by the choice of David) has proved vital if the energy that will be released is the energy God wants to release.

At the *intuitive* level I have not found it difficult to give others responsibility and authority. A former staff member once asked me, 'Which do you find more difficult, handing something over to others and seeing them do it worse than you, or seeing them do it better than you?' It was a very good question, which all leaders can benefit from asking themselves. My own response was that I had no problem seeing others do things better, but that I did struggle when I saw things being done badly.

Facing those times when mistakes have been made in delegation is essential. They can become important learning points. Sometimes the very extent of a person's commitment to a task has had harmful side effects, such as producing an empire mentality and a possessiveness about that area of ministry. This is often painful to confront and deal with, particularly when caused by some unresolved inner problem that may well have been brought to the surface through the giving of responsibility. A person may be serving others in order to gain attention, to get power, to exercise control, or to make a good impression. When any of these things happen, the leader's role is primarily pastoral; helping the person concerned to face the hidden emotional agenda in their lives which has come to the surface.

What is happening often in such a situation is that God is taking the person onto the anvil of experience in order to shape them. Only in so far as we have gone that way before them can we help such a person to allow God to act. If we have kept ourselves hidden from God's purposes and the change and growth he desires to bring about in us then we will inevitably either collude with another person in their hiding from God, or we will communicate a judging attitude by requiring others to go where we have not been willing to venture. Either way the real problem will not be resolved, but rather projected onto the surrounding situation – that usually means onto other people. We remain unhealed, so do those we lead, and then our brokenness is projected onto the church. No wonder, when this happens, that our witness to the redemption of creation which Christ has brought to the world, and desires to be incarnate in the church, has a hollow ring.

In these situations we have to exercise faith and patience so as not to run too quickly to the help of others. They have hit a growing point, and God is disturbing them into life. They will often be tempted to avoid that confrontation with God by projecting their troubles onto us.

When this happens, concerned friends of the person may come, sometimes with considerable aggression, with the accusing question: 'Why isn't the church doing something to help?' The fact is that the Holy Spirit is doing spiritual and emotional surgery – indeed, open heart surgery, we might call it. It is no help if we assist such people to find out how to get off the operating table. Yes, we can give comfort and support and should do so, but not in a way that helps them avoid the creative pain. As Leanne Payne has said, 'The pain is part of the healing.' Jesus's strongest words of rebuke to Peter took place when he was trying to find a way to help Jesus avoid the pain of the cross.

Those who cannot see what is going on will almost inevitably focus their frustration and anger onto us. Fulfilling the role of scapegoat is, in my experience, a non-negotiable element of helping others, and a whole church, to grow. However, Jesus has shown it to be profoundly creative. When we go that way we will know his presence in what feels like a wilderness of misunderstanding and misrepresentation. It is a painful path that tests our own wholeness, but it can be life-giving to others as they break through their emotional barriers into the next stage of wholeness for them.

As long as we recognise that we too are only pilgrims on the pathway to maturity, and are facing the points of challenge to us as people, it is usually possible to help another fellow traveller on the road to see and seize the opportunity to grow, rather than to have an even more painful task of taking responsibility from someone. When this happens, the energy released in delegation is harnessed not only for the transference and extension of vision, but also for the growth into wholeness in those to whom the work has been delegated. By this means truth becomes incarnate in our lives.

Practical Framework
Principally because I am quite comfortable with delegating many things to others (an *intuitive* state), I have had to work hard on the *analytical* side to ensure that when I delegate I do the job well by monitoring it properly. This is a subtle art and skill, and I have found it helpful to develop a check list to help ensure that I am doing it as well as I know how.

Someone has said, 'Marriage is like twirling a baton, turning handsprings, or eating with chopsticks; it looks easy till you try it.' The same can be said of delegation; which is why I have developed a simple analytical tool which has been a great help in ensuring that I am delegating to the best of my ability. I created this myself having realised that I was not doing the work of delegation well simply by relying on my intuition.

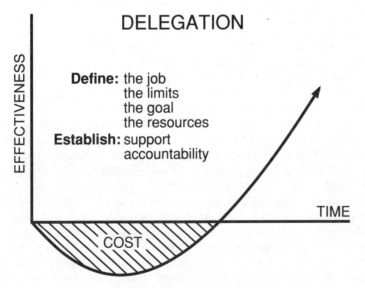

Delegation diagram and check list

I have superimposed a check list onto a graph which plots effectiveness against time to remind me, and others, that there is a cost to delegation. Effectiveness may well go down in the short term, and can cause extra work as well. That is the difficulty with delegation. It is often quicker, in the short run, to do the job myself. The most effective thing in the long run, however, is to delegate to others; always remembering that supervision, assessment and accountability will remain residual responsibilities. A delegated responsibility should still involve me in some work. If it involves me in no work then I have abdicated, not delegated. Thus the person who says, 'I am working myself out of a job' has usually not learned to delegate, because delegation involves continuing to work with the person to whom we have given the task. That work may well start with a fairly directive approach, but should increasingly give the person space to develop – and implement – their own solutions.

Gradually we can move from trainer to supporter – and it is even possible for the roles to be reversed and for us to end up as learners. For that to happen we need to be sufficiently open to God for him to be able to draw to our attention and deal with any sense of threat we might feel. This is all part of what it means to be on the anvil of experience.

The whole operation of delegation should involve a continuing process of ebb and flow, recognising that sometimes it is necessary to move backwards in the flow of delegation, when things are not going well. My experience suggests that it is best to avoid dramatic swings and changes if at all possible.

Effectiveness not only relates to time but also to how well each element in the check list has been established. To aid this I now usually define on paper for clarity, the job; the limits; the goal; the resources; the support, and the accountability.

Obviously the first thing to define is the *job*. It may be something obvious like 'edit the parish magazine', or something rather more abstract like 'monitor the church's prayer life'. The *limits* also need defining, which may include time and money, as well as some definition of the boundaries. For example, in the case of the editor of the magazine this would include the limits of editorial control. I have found that defining such limits in advance reduces conflict later, simply because no two people's perception of what is appropriate or not ever seems to be the same. I know what I mean by editing the magazine, but I do not mean authority to print personal attacks on the archbishop or articles supporting the Moonies. It is as well to define that before we begin. The limits would also include a definition of how long the job is being taken on for. We always have a defined term for any job in the life of the church, so that we and the person involved know the limits of the task. Neither they, nor we, will be trapped for ever.

The *goal* is about the job's purpose. In the case of the magazine it is important to know whether it is intended primarily as a means of informing the church members about what is happening in the church, or communicating the faith to non-church members, or something in between. To delegate is to find something done differently, which is why defining what it is that we want done is so vital. Next come the *resources* which the person can expect to draw on in order to do the job. What money they can spend, how much time they can expect to spend with me, what office staff – if any – they can draw on for help, what access to the congregation they can have to publicise the work and draw others in.

When all these items have been identified, I then go on to establish two other important matters. First, is the level and nature of *support* which the person can expect. Their ideas and mine may be very different. 'I would be happy to spend an hour a month talking over your plans for the magazine for the first year until you no longer feel you need that much help' is how I might approach this matter with the editor of the magazine. It will reduce future hassle if we agree what is acceptable to both before we begin. I also then establish the *accountability* which the person has to me or someone else. I may want to review how things are going once a term, and for us to report to the church council once every year, so that they can make comments on the effectiveness of what is being done and make suggestions about improvements.

Rich Rewards
I have written about the complexities of learning to pray as a church, of establishing a creative dialogue between leaders and

church members, and of becoming proficient in delegation, so that vision may be transferred and the whole church 'buy into' the direction that has been discerned to be from God. In these complexities we have continued to see the dynamic interplay of *inspiration*, *intuition* and *analysis* in each of these elements of transferring the vision.

However, the picture is not complete without reference to the rich rewards that are to be found on the path of an effective transfer of vision to the whole membership of a group or organisation or church. It is the difference between the sun and moon, seeing people fired from within rather than simply reflecting the vision of another person. A whole community energised, and given both the freedom and skills needed to serve God, is a joy to behold. People grow beyond recognition when given the space to act, and enough support to be able to learn from their mistakes. The life of any such church will prosper because an army has been mobilised. The kingdom of God will be manifested in ways which can surprise even the leader.

One little incident which happened to me recently encapsulates these rewards. I have now delegated leadership of each of our four congregations to other staff members; together with the welcome of newcomers which is delegated to welcome teams in each of those congregations. One Sunday I was sitting among a congregation for one of the services. There was a lady sitting next to me whom I did not know, and so I spoke to her after the service. I discovered that she had moved into the area six months before, and – due to the break-up of her marriage – had been seeking both company and meaning in life. She had begun to attend St Thomas's. The welcome team had introduced themselves and helped her to make friends and to begin to consider the implications of the Christian faith. I innocently asked her what had been happening to her faith since she had begun worshipping at this church. 'Plenty,' she replied, 'I became a Christian last week, so this Sunday is a special one for me!' I rejoiced with her, and was just about to move on to prepare myself to lead the following service, when she turned to me and said: 'I've told you about myself, but who are you?'

Such are the joys of learning how to hear the call of God to 'let my people go', and its twin 'let my people grow'.

Chapter Seven

IMPLEMENTING CHANGE

At one particularly testing time in our building project I remember thinking about how Moses might have felt as he led the
children of Israel out over dry ground across the Red Sea. It must
have been amazingly exciting to realise that the way out of the
troubles was through a miracle of parting the waters ('We've
never done this before, vicar!'). Maybe even that paled into
insignificance with the thrill of actually seeing the waters part.
Yet I wonder if – perhaps about halfway – a sinking feeling hit
him as his emotions settled down. Like a cold shower of reality,
did he for a moment wonder if he might be the only one crossing?
Was everyone else standing on the safety of the river bank
roaring with laughter – watching as the waters rushed towards
him? Certainly there have been such moments in my ministry
when, after the excitement of sensing God's call, we have then
begun to move to implement that vision, and the feelings involved became very different. The willingness to go through this
pain barrier has been vital.

It is one thing to have a vision of what could be: it is quite
another matter to bring that vision into reality. Bringing about
change is probably the toughest part of any leadership role – yet
one of the most important. Without change, stagnation and
irrelevance creep into any group or organisation. Change in the
church has often seemed to me like handling an ocean-going
liner. The engines need to be started and working under considerable power before any movement is detected. But once

change has begun to happen it has, like the liner, a momentum all of its own.

During a time of considerable change, we did a survey of the church and included questions about the two major changes we were introducing. One was the introduction of a 'signs and wonders' approach to the healing ministry, and the other was the introduction of the nine o'clock service as our outreach to the urban youth culture.

Fascinatingly the response to both questions was almost identical. In each case eighty-four per cent agreed, forty per cent of them strongly. The remaining sixteen per cent were divided equally between those who did not have an opinion, those who disagreed, and those who strongly disagreed. I hasten to add that this was not done to establish whether our theology was right, but whether we had the support of the church. What the survey showed was that the church had a positive attitude to change – almost regardless of what it was we were implementing. There has not always been such confidence in our leadership. It has come about only after a decade or more of leading the church into a largely positive experience of change. Many lessons have had to be learned about what enables change, despite the huge uncertainties it can cause, to become a positive experience.

Learning to Wait

Paradoxically, the primary lesson I have learned about discovering God's inspiration for moving into change in the church has had to do with learning to wait. Preaching one harvest festival about the patience of the farmer uncovered an important biblical truth for me. I had taken the text:

> Be patient, then, brothers, until the Lord's coming. See how the farmer waits for the land to yield its valuable crop and how patient he is for the autumn and spring rains. You too, be patient and stand firm, because the Lord's coming is near.

(Jas 5.7,8)

'Waiting' has gained a negative connotation. We have all experienced times, especially as children, when 'wait' did not mean 'not yet', but rather 'not at all, although I do not intend to say that right now'. Waiting was an easy way of saying no –

without saying no. Moreover, in our highly mechanical and electrical world so much of our experience tells us that waiting is pointless. We live in a culture with an allergy to waiting.

The world of agriculture has a different perspective. The farmer, as he seeks to co-operate with powers beyond his control (the sun, the seed, the rain and the soil), knows that his job is all about waiting. Waiting for the right moment to sow, and waiting for the right moment to harvest. So it is in the work of the kingdom, which Jesus so often spoke of in agricultural terms. We have to learn the art of waiting for God's action if we are to see effective change brought about. These are three ways in which this works out.

First, we have to wait for the vision. Without vision there is no divine empowering to move forward. This is why the previous two chapters have been devoted to the subject of discovering and transferring vision. The presupposition of this chapter is that we have that vision from God.

Second, we have to wait for the call of God to be heard by gifted leaders. Without such leaders we will make little or no progress. But it is worth waiting for them to hear the call themselves, for the call of God is the best motivation there is. Even then it may be a hard battle to clear the decks for that motivation to have breathing space.

Shortly after my experience of charismatic renewal I realised that the 'fuel' on which the church was running was moral duty reinforced by moral pressure. The need constituted the call. No one thought of saying no to a request by the vicar to take on a job. That was helpful in the short run in getting jobs done, but I saw how contrary to the gospel it was. Here we were as an evangelical church committed to proclaiming justification by grace, yet our method of operating was salvation by good works.

Seeing a gap in the leadership of our children's work, I went to someone in the church and invited her to consider it. By then, I had learned that I had to do this by asking her to pray and see if God was telling her to take it on. She came back with a surprising answer. She saw the need, but for the first time in twenty years as a believer in Christian work, she was going to dare to say no. The need did not constitute the call. The message was getting through and I affirmed her in this step: an important milestone in her growth as a person which, having the care of her soul, was my first calling.

Unfortunately, it left a gap of considerable proportions.

The next person I approached (and the only other person I saw as possibly able to take on this work) knew this was not God's call and said so very speedily. Too speedily as it happened. As I was wondering what on earth to do next, heaven was opening the windows. It happened through a dream which this second person had in which she saw herself in the centre of a group of children and knowing that she was meant to be there. She came back to me and said she now had God's call and was ready to take on the work. Her three years' leadership has been one of the outstanding periods in our children's work through which we have been amazed at how real God has become to five- and six-year-olds. Truly it is all done by grace: but grace is a seemingly risky path for the leader seeking to 'get on with the job'. Yet it is the call of God alone that brings about vision, motivation, incredible creativity and sacrifice. It is worth working, waiting and watching for.

Third, we have had to learn to wait for God's moment to act. It is one thing to have a vision, but quite another to know the right time to act on it. I first learned this lesson from Michael Baughen when I worked as his curate. He had a strong and persistent vision for the establishing of a men's group. This was despite the fact that such groups were dwindling in size and in number across the country. Strong though the vision was, Michael waited three years before acting. When the time came – and a gifted leader had been 'given' – the group was quickly launched and grew to close on one hundred members in a matter of months. It was God's moment to act.

The same lesson has been repeated endlessly. I had become convinced by January 1985 that dividing the church into 'congregations' was the way ahead. Yet at that stage I could not even carry my churchwardens with me. It made me go through the whole idea again to see if I had mistaken the vision. I was convinced I had not. Rather than launch into high levels of conflict I judged that what was wrong was the timing. It was not until two and a half years later that the vision became reality. By then we went ahead unitedly.

Leadership is a matter of timing. To revert to the farming

picture, if you harvest too early the grain is not fully developed and if you wait too long heavy rain may have destroyed the whole crop. To act too early is likely to result in a divided church; to wait too long will result in a de-motivated church which has lost enthusiasm. Like surfing, the art is in catching the wave just before it breaks.

The great temptation is to harvest too early. We have a vision and then act as though that made all careful planning and research redundant. The truth is that it makes them all the more vital. Time, as well as money, needs to be spent on employing an architect to do a feasibility study *before* we can be sure the vision is of God. We need to spend money on research and development before we can be sure of the way ahead. Effort needs to be spent in going over the arguments endlessly so that the whole church has bought into the vision. The waiting time is vital and creative. One of the most important principles I have learned about implementing change is summed up in the saying 'softly softly catchee monkey'!

Holding on and Coming Back

Two other lessons I have learned about discovering God's inspiration for change are to do with holding on to the vision in the process of waiting, and learning to return to the place of past failures. 'If the vision tarries, wait for it,' says the prophet. James, in the passage quoted, draws the lesson of waiting with the words, 'You too be patient and stand firm.' The temptation

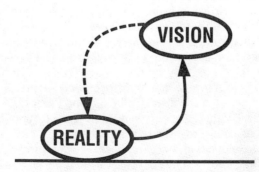

Holding on to vision when reality is different

however is to compromise the vision, as Abraham did when God's promise of a child seemed long past possibility of fulfilment. This can be illustrated diagrammatically (see page 107).

Vision is about a reality yet to be. There is therefore a creative tension between what is and what will be. What is so tempting is to pull vision down to our reality (*the dotted line*). The youth leader begins with great enthusiasm to seek to help young people to come to maturity, in faith and as people. He may find such pressure over discipline problems, however, that he ends up working with the vision simply of keeping the building in one piece. Or, for example, the leader of a home group has a vision, perhaps to get the group to be out-going, but lets go of it simply because everyone around wants to hold on to the reality that the group is a comfortable place to be.

In the final issue the leader is accountable to God and needs to be faithful to his calling if reality is to move towards vision (*the solid line*). Prayer and sheer dogged endurance are needed to hold on, and perhaps to do even more – to have the courage to return to the scene of past failures. So many of the major steps forward at St Thomas's have been the result of looking failure in the face, owning it for what it was, and looking to God for answers. This has become so much a part of our experience that I now consciously look for the failure points, for their potential to be the areas where we will next see a move forward.

For example, out of the demise of our uniformed organisations has arisen the development of youth work with a full-time worker and part-time assistant. Out of the demise of our robed choir has arisen now five worship teams who play a vital part in enabling the church to enter into God's presence in worship. Out of our admission that the geographical grouping of fellowship groups into 'areas' had not worked came the present structure of 'congregations'.

At each point faith has had to be exercised because there has been a gap between the death of the old and the resurrection of the new. I call it the Easter eve syndrome. It is so tempting to fill the gap, but almost invariably we fill it with our ideas and not God's. That only sets his purposes back. We need both to hold on and to believe for this ability to bring forth a miracle, as Abraham eventually did.

Stepping Out

Three lessons, which I have entered into intuitively, stand out for me in this matter of helping a church to change.

First, there is an unavoidable element of 'going out in front' for the leader of any group which is having to tackle change. The Duke of Plaza Toro was the man who 'led his regiment from behind – he found it less exciting'! What we do in leadership, however, is not primarily about what the leader feels comfortable with, but is about what will best bring about the coming of God's kingdom. For that, there are times when we need to be men and women of action.

The fine Christian writer G. K. Chesterton was a plump man. During the war he was giving a lecture when a militant woman stood up, accused him of being a coward, and shouted out, 'Mr Chesterton, sir, you should be out at the Front.' Without a moment's hesitation he replied, 'Madam, if you come round to the side you will see that I am already out at the front!'

Being 'out at the front' is certainly what I have found leadership to be all about. The leader who will not pay that price will be the poorer, as will be the work he leads. There are times when the leader simply has to say, with Martin Luther, 'Here I stand, I can do no other,' or rather, with Jesus he has to say, 'Follow me.'

Experience has written this into my present attitude to leadership in many ways. Arriving at St Thomas's and finding the worship pattern a frustration, I knew I had to stick my neck out and say, 'This is the way' about joining the two morning services into one. Similarly, nearly twenty years later, I saw that it was necessary to say, 'This is the way' about developing 'congregations' and dividing the one morning service into two.

Whether it is Moses crossing the Red Sea, or Paul making a collection for the Christians in Jerusalem, the Scriptures are full of this form of 'up front' leadership. It is costly, for we need to know the mind of God enough to have confidence that this is his way.

During the building project we came home from holiday to discover that the deed had been done – the chancel and vestries had been demolished. In their place stood a gaping hole. It was a moment of truth which sent a shiver down my spine when I saw it.

It seemed so destructive of all that worshippers had valued over nearly a century. Was this really of God? Within a week I had a member of the congregation coming to tell me that God had told her that we were wrong to turn the building around, and that he was saying we should put it all back! I needed confidence in the rightness of what we were doing at that point. That confidence was something which the church needed to carry it through the high risk of the project. That is the cost of God's call to leadership.

Breaking the Emotional Barrier

One of the lasting gains of charismatic renewal within the church has been openness and honesty about feelings. This has altered the climate in which discussions and decisions about change have taken place. We have been able to look the hidden agenda in the face – to identify why we feel as we do, and how that affects our approach to some issue. Once the feelings are owned they can be dealt with. When they are not admitted they have a much more profound, and usually destructive, effect on the outcome. Discovering this led me into *the second intuitive insight: seeking to break through, rather than be constricted by, emotional barriers to change, both in myself and others.*

I have learned to treat emotions rather like money. Rather than start, in the building project, by asking how much money we had and then making plans accordingly, we did our work the other way round. First we sought to discover the will of God, then we trusted him with the financial needs, and concluded by making the sacrifices we were called to make to bring the vision about. We have learned to treat emotions in the same way. First we identify what changes we are being called upon to make. We then take an 'emotional audit', by seeking to anticipate what people might or do feel about such change. We then look for a way, not of coming up with a more acceptable plan, but of giving the emotional support to enable people to cope with the change.

Sometimes the emotional support has come through the use of humour. People who were anxious about turning the church to face west were told, 'We are still facing east – it is just that it is the long way round.' This helped them to see the funny side of the anxiety they had.

Another small incident, about the sort of cups we should have, probably had a profound effect on the attitudes within the church. It happened soon after I arrived when the church council had agreed to serve coffee in church after services. We needed new cups. Many on the council were in favour of asking everyone to bring old cups they no longer needed. I was offended by such attitudes to God. Further discussion produced the rationale for such an approach, that if we purchased good quality cups then people would take them. We quickly got into discussion about what we might have stamped on them to avoid theft. 'Stolen from St Thomas's' was my favoured inscription! The atmosphere relaxed, and the cups were purchased. It was a little point but probably prepared the way for the policy of 'only the best is good enough for God' which was foundational to the way we approached the building project.

More often the emotional support needed has led us into a counselling situation and to the heart of the gospel, namely personal growth. A person who is highly agitated about some change may feel threatened by a loss of power or a feeling of insecurity. It is those matters, not the changes envisaged, which need to be confronted. Such changes all too frequently uncover a need to control, or the building of a personal empire. Such matters need to be confronted not accepted, in order for the kingdom to come for the individual concerned and for the whole church. It is in this way that emotional barriers are overcome. Doing so has helped individuals grow and the whole church to extend its effectiveness.

Open Government
The third intuitive insight into the management of change has to do with an open form of church government. I found myself talking freely with church members about thoughts and ideas which were going around my mind and began to analyse why I was working the way I was. I came to several conclusions.

First, I did not feel possessive about ideas. If they were mine they were also public property and everyone was entitled to support, attack, or improve on them. If they were ideas that other people had, I did not feel threatened by their source.

Second, I discovered that knocking ideas about is a vital part of discerning the will of God. If an idea is of God the process of criticising and weighing it will only sharpen the outline and confirm God's leading. If it is not, then analysis will either demolish it or cause it to melt into the background and be forgotten.

Third, as a result, ideas are genuinely welcomed – including criticism. Those criticisms are usually constructive, but where they have a personal barb to them (which is rare indeed) I have learned to ignore the emotions and listen to the criticism. They often have a valid point, which if listened to can add to the effectiveness of what we are doing.

In these ways the membership feels listened to and their contribution valued. When that happens I have also discovered that the need of everyone to have their way on everything is reduced. It is enough to be heard. Important in this is the communication that the vicar's ideas are no more sacred than other people's. It is all right to disagree. I certainly do not win the argument all the time.

Releasing Constraints

It was David Wasdell who introduced me to Lewin's force field. I first saw it represented by the use of an old picture frame with a central wooden knob held in place by strong elastic bands radiating from the corners and centres of each side.

David explained that the knob was held in the centre of balancing forces (in this case, the equal tension of each elastic strand). This he likened to a community of people (a church, for example), which has forces making for growth and forces making for decline in it.

One way in which growth is often sought is by tying a piece of string around the knob and pulling hard. This is like someone from outside, such as an evangelist, coming in and giving a great boost to the place – but only temporarily. The problem is that as soon as that outside help has gone, everything reverts to where it was, or even bounces back further in the opposite direction for a while. In fact, while such a person has been here, all the forces working for constraint have been at full stretch. Those represent-ing the 'go-ahead' element, by contrast, have been abdicating

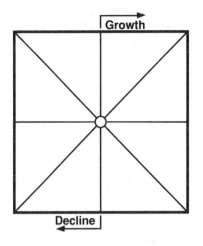

Lewin's force field

responsibility by leaving it to the missioner, and sitting back and enjoying the ride.

Another way to move the whole structure towards growth is to pull hard on one or more of the growth strings. In practice this means encouraging those working for growth to such an extent that their combined pressure will win the opposition over. However, what we now have are two virtually equal and opposite forces, both in a place of tension. The more you pull on growth, the stronger the resistance you will find to change.

The most effective way of securing lasting change, however, is to release the constraints: to take the pressure off the forces working for decline. If we get those 'forces working for decline' in our hand, and help them to let go, then everything moves naturally in the direction of growth.

What this has meant in practice is that once a problem is identified, we need to go on to identify what the constraints are. When we know those, we can begin to facilitate changes. The trouble is that Christian leaders tend to do the opposite: working too readily on the 'argument weak, shout loudest' principle. If the church is failing to give, or evangelise, or grow, or whatever is our goal, we all too easily shout and put people under moral

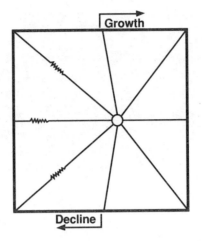

Releasing constraints

pressure. Sadly this tends to create more problems than it solves. Before we had an unmotivated group. Now we have an unmotivated and guilty group, which is no great advance!

A recent example of releasing constraints at St Thomas's came about when we noticed that the growth of the church had not been reflected in the size of our Christmas carol services. Rather than berating the church for not inviting others, we started asking what the constraints were. Eventually we discerned that there was confusion about the purpose of these services. As leaders we saw them as one of the great opportunities to invite non-church people. The church, however, perceived that the way we were running such services indicated that our goal was to serve the church, and thereby cut the community out. The church responded by doing just that – not inviting the community.

Now we have identified this we have been able to spell out what our goal is, who the services are aimed at, and how we intend to handle them. Our experience would suggest – unless there is something we have missed – that within three years we should have built a new 'tradition' of carol services which will have the confidence of the congregation. By then there should be evidence in the numbers coming.

One of the enormous gains of seeking to release constraints is that the church tends to be drawn together in unity. Those committed to growth and advance in the particular area are excited that the problem is being faced. They also begin to see that there are some problems in the way that they had not honestly faced before. Those who are reluctant to change, or resistant to it, often begin to relax and become less threatened because it is their fears and objections which are being talked about, listened to and faced. Separated, these two groups will achieve little – except to fall apart. Together, it is possible to face the fears and fulfil the hopes – if we learn to look at, and then release, the constraints.

Pulling Together
In bringing about effective and lasting change we have re-peatedly discovered that all three elements in the framework for learning need to be active and working well together. Nowhere was this more evident than in the profound yet subtle changes we had to make in breaking through the 'two hundred barrier' which many churches struggle to surmount.

The usual pattern is for church membership to grow to around two hundred and then to level out. For every person added by 'mission', one is lost by 'omission' – a feeling of being ignored or no longer significant.

Analysis, in the form of church growth theory and our own statistics, first alerted us to this barrier. The principles of releas-ing constraints have given us a tool with which to manage the change needed. We also brought the matter before God in prayer for his *inspiration*, and began to feel our way *intuitively* to a way through the impasse. Grouping the fellowship groups together in geographical areas was the intuitive idea which caught the im-agination of much of the leadership as we prayed about it. By the time we looked around we were already up to five hundred members a Sunday.

In retrospect, several points are worth making. First, the structure got us through the barrier but was not a long-term solution. What had been a help had to be discarded in due course. Second, it has probably taken us ten years, with a considerable amount of trial and error, to find the appropriate way to multiply pastoral oversight. This is essential if growth is to be maintained. Third, major emotional changes had to be made by all of us. For myself, changing from 'caring for everyone' to 'ensuring everyone is cared for' felt like the shepherd abandoning the sheep: it certainly confronted me with my need to be needed, which had to be dealt with in the process.

For the congregation the change was highlighted by one deliberately humorous point in a sermon preached during the changes. The subject was Jethro's advice to Moses about sharing responsibility. The curate, who was preaching, then made the point that whereas in the past you might have been honoured by a visit by the vicar, you now needed to realise that only the 'hard cases were dealt with by Moses'. 'This means,' he added, 'that Robert will only be coming to see you if everyone else has despaired of you!' It was overstating the case to make the point – but it is remembered to this day.

We are having to hold together *intuition*, *inspiration* and *analysis* just as much today, as we face new problems and challenges in order to continue to grow past the one thousand worshippers level. The problems seem much bigger, but we have been this way before. Implementing the changes which will be necessary will be no easier than in the past. Yet the insights gained from past experience suggest that these changes, despite all that they will mean, can be received as a positive experience.

Personal Agenda
'Everyone talks of changing the world, but no one talks of changing himself,' said Leo Tolstoy. The truth is that implementing change will only happen freely and fruitfully where personal growth and change are taking place in the leader. Professor John Adair is quoted as saying that, in industry, no man can effectively bring about change who is not willing himself to be changed. That is also true in the life of a church. This is why the leader needs to be allowing God to take him onto the anvil of experience in order that he might grow as a person. As we co-operate with this process we will ourselves be equipped to bring about change in others. It is a high cost, but also a holy calling.

Chapter Eight

TAKING PEOPLE WITH YOU

There is an apocryphal story of a clergyman who, while saying his prayers, was visited by an angel. The angel said that he was allowed to ask any question he wished about the life hereafter. The clergyman, a cricketing enthusiast, asked: 'Is there cricket in heaven?' The angel was stumped by this question and had to admit that he (or she!) did not know the answer and would have to go away and find it out. Two weeks later the angel visited the clergyman again during his prayers. 'I have the answer to your question, and there is both good and bad news for you,' he said. 'The good news is that there is cricket in heaven.' 'Well what can be the bad news, then?' asked the clergyman. 'You are on tonight!' the angel announced.

Although I have never been visited by an angel, I know that sense of 'being on tonight', which inevitably happens when we seek to lead other people into the fulfilment of a vision. This is the crunch moment for leaders. It is essential if the vision we have sought after is to find fulfilment. Often this is the greatest question for leaders: how can we take people with us? It is this question we now need to address.

Ted Engstrom, in his book *The Making of a Christian Leader*, writes: 'When God creates a leader, he gives him the capacity to make things happen.' In my experience that is not given in full measure at the moment of commissioning or ordination. Rather it is the fruit of the costly process of incarnational learning. That is God's primary means of equipping us. This, of course, is good news for most of us leaders. We rarely feel that we 'have what it takes' to lead the particular group we are responsible for, and it is good news indeed that God is able to equip us. He is committed to give that equipping to all who will receive it. The 'bad' news is that if we are to receive it, the process must be allowed to touch us at the core of our being. Especially is this so when we move out into the public arena to put our vision into practice, still wondering whether it really is of God, whether it will actually work, and whether we have the sheer ability to take people with us.

Learning to Love
If the key to changing the church is learning to wait, as I have argued in the previous chapter, the key to taking others with us can seem equally contradictory at first sight, for it involves letting them go free! Painful experience, and prayerful reflection, have both been needed for me to understand why this is so. However in this I have come to understand more of what is involved in God's *inspiration* for the effective motivation of others.

Part of the struggle which preceded the 'dark night of the soul' I have already referred to, had to do with a need to achieve. I was highly motivated to make things happen. However, it was a draining experience done, as I now see, in the energy of the flesh. I was brought up with a start while studying Isaiah 58 which contains the salutary words: 'In the day of your festivals you oppress all your workers.' I was using others (albeit in the cause of the gospel) to meet my need for acceptance and approval.

It was not difficult to see that such need-induced industry is hardly capable of working the works of God. I had to let go: and be willing to fail. Renewal had been a deep experience of the grace, the free and unmerited love, of God. I now saw that the church needed to be built on grace. The means and the ends must proclaim the same message: God has come to set us free – including from ourselves. On the anvil of experience God can write this truth into us and so enable us to help others travel the same path.

Since that time I have been continually brought to that place of openness before God to see whether my own motivation is his glory or my need. Only the former is good news for the church. I now see it as one of the greatest occupational hazards of the ministry: fooling ourselves about our motives. How often do we ministers say to our spouses, 'I must just do this, or go there' without stopping to consider where the 'must' comes from. Is it the call of God or my needs?

Out of that experience has come the recognition of the need to help others to be true in their motivation. This is not only for their well-being, important though that is, but it is also vital if I am to take people with me for the right reasons. The only true motivation, by the yardstick of the life of Jesus, is love which is freely given and which demands no repayment. All ministry is geared to helping people live, as measured by the fullness of life Jesus exhibited. Leading others involves helping them in their being as well as their doing: the latter growing out of the former. This was the new direction I had received in my service of others.

Building by Grace

It was this experience which prepared me for prayerful reflection on the comment of a businessman in the congregation. It was his chance remark that brought my thinking into focus. Half jokingly he said that he was glad to be in a work environment where you had more control of people's actions and behaviour than you do in a voluntary society where it all seems to depend on 'psyching people up to do things'.

I have never liked thinking of the church as a 'voluntary society', but I had to acknowledge that this is an accurate description of it in terms of motivation. Unlike a totalitarian society or military organisation, we do not have the power to control the lives of others: though it is the mark of the cults to motivate people in just that way. Nor do we have the controlling influence of money (and with it the right to 'hire and fire') which is how the commercial world operates. Yet, thinking about that word 'voluntary' led me back to reconsider our experience during the building project of how people had been motivated to give. 'Voluntary', from its Latin root, actually means 'willing', and one crucial text had taught us more than any other about how to handle the motivation of the church to give willingly with great generosity:

> Each man should give what he has decided in his heart to give, not reluctantly or under compulsion, for God loves a cheerful giver.
>
> (2 Cor 9.7)

We had tried setting goals for individual giving but discovered two ways in which it was not effective. It always felt like law and so cut out the dimension of love to God in giving. Moreover it never seemed to motivate: rather it immobilised by freezing people in guilt. So we let go of such an approach and simply urged people to pray and give. What happened as a result was breathtaking. Generosity overflowed. People were choosing freely, and the floodgates of giving swung wide open on such a hinge.

Having grasped this principle in the area of giving it was then possible to apply it in all other areas in the life of the church – not least in the matter of the active service that members were involved in. We abandoned attempts to motivate people through a sense of guilt or duty, or out of the pressure of the need. Rather we encouraged everyone who was considering taking on some task to seek God's will in the matter. It often leaves us with gaps that we have to trust to God, but it has produced a harvest of willing servants.

Consequently I have come to the conclusion that willing service is what makes a venture of any kind one which reflects the nature of the service of Christ, who freely and willingly gave himself. I believe there are implications in this conclusion for the whole of human life. Totalitarian states can command people and despots can coerce people through fear; but neither can motivate others. As I write, some of the countries of Eastern Europe are being given their first opportunity since the second world war to choose their government. Their voting reveals that communism has won very few hearts. You cannot by-pass the individual's choice. A free response of love is what 'voluntary' means. For this reason, I rejoice to be working as a leader in a voluntary society, because without people's free choice being involved we have not begun to enter into what I now believe leadership to be truly about.

Developing Trust

No leader of others can be totally unaware of how those people are responding, especially as it is on the quality of that response that the effectiveness of what is being attempted depends. However, self-delusion can limit the degree of awareness! Nonetheless, for those wanting to increase their awareness of how things are going, *intuition* is a vital tool which can demonstrate how effectiveness can be improved.

Three things stand out for me as intuitive yardsticks which can make or break our ability to take people with us.

First, *confidence* needs to be established. I find it fascinating to consider the elements that went to make up King David's authority in Israel. God had called him, and he had been anointed by Samuel – and the Holy Spirit – for such a leadership role. Yet, even when Saul and Jonathan were dead, David did not seize power or claim it as his right. He waited for the people to invite and accept him.

> All the tribes of Israel came to David at Hebron and said, 'We are your own flesh and blood. In the past while Saul was king over us, you were the one who led Israel on their military campaigns. And the Lord said to you, "You shall shepherd my people Israel, and you shall become their ruler."'
> When all the elders of Israel had come to King David at Hebron, the king made a compact with them at Hebron before the Lord, and they anointed David king over Israel.
>
> (2 Sam 5.1–3)

Anointed by God, and victorious in battle, David yet understood that he needed the willing acceptance of the people. That takes time, especially if the leader is drafted in from outside the situation, as David was. There is a vital process of bonding between the congregation (or group) and the leader which is made more demanding if the person is appointed from outside the group or church. This is not an argument against appointing leaders in this way, but rather it is a recognition of the dynamic of bonding between a leader and those he leads. An important part in that process is the modern equivalent of winning your spurs, which can only happen when the new leader is put in a testing situation. How he deals with it will determine whether or not people will give themselves to his leadership or not.

I was fortunate (at least in retrospect), in moving to Sheffield, to have a quick opportunity for such testing because of my perception that the church was ready to change the pattern of Sunday worship. It was a vital opportunity to show, by action, that I was able to lead, and through this gain my spurs.

I am increasingly convinced that the normal, often soothing, words of new leaders about not changing anything for six months is a foolish promise that could cause a unique opportunity to make significant changes to be missed. Indeed, why have a new leader if there is to be nothing new? Good leadership involves exercising the courage to lead, and that will involve making changes.

However, it was not long before I felt as if I had not just lost my spurs, but my horse as well! While my becoming involved in charismatic renewal created only a little, though very vocal, conflict it engendered a much more widespread hesitation and 'pulling back' of the whole congregation. Everyone seemed to stand back and watch what happened. If there was to be an explosion they did not want to be too near. In the providence of God another crucial testing time came with the launch in 1972 of our first gift day for £1,250. The overwhelming response, of over £3,000, again renewed confidence in my leadership. I could sense the rush of wind as the whole church seemed to 'come back in' emotionally: even though there had been little or no change in anything outward like attendance or giving.

There is no value in looking for crises to respond to – indeed, the chances are that they will come to you before you have the chance to look for them! When an issue confronts us early on in leadership then we need to choose to face it. Confront it clearly, think it through well (faith is no substitute for thought), and where you sense the leading of God act decisively. It will prove crucial for that subsequent free giving of loyalty from others. Like love it can never be demanded or required, only won and given – freely.

Loyalty is another essential ingredient for effective leadership to be exercised. It only comes as a result of establishing real personal relationships with those we are leading: knowing them and caring for them as people. It is not easy to define, but it is essential to have. People need to feel valued and accepted if they are to operate effectively. On one of the plaques on the walls of the church is a commemoration of the first curate of St Thomas's who died shortly after leaving Crookes to be vicar of Goole just over one hundred years ago. At the bottom of the plaque is the sentence:

'He was loved for his own sake, and for his work's sake.'

That has always seemed to me to have love and ministry in the right order. However, there is a 'down-side' to such relationships. When the task has been finished and the leader establishes a new relationship with the person they are now working with, the one who has stood down can feel doubly bereft. They have handed over the task, and lost a valued relationship. I have been slow to see the depth of bereavement this causes and am only just beginning to address it when people change tasks within the church.

King David had obviously established this sort of quality of personal relationship with his leadership team, judging by their response to him:

> Three of the thirty chiefs came down to David to the rock at the cave of Adullam, while a band of Philistines was encamped in the Valley of Rephaim. At that time David was in the stronghold, and the Philistine garrison was at Bethlehem. David longed for water and said: 'Oh, that someone would get me a drink of water from the well near the gate of Bethlehem!' So the three broke through the Philistine lines, drew water from the well near the gate of Bethlehem and carried it back to David.
>
> (1 Chron 11.15–18)

Besides confidence and loyalty, the third intuitive yardstick by which to measure how well we are leading others, is what I can only describe as *humanity*. Rather than humanity I first wrote the words 'develop a limp', because of Jacob's wrestling with God which left him both blessed by God but also aware of his human frailty.

So many biblical leaders had such an encounter with God through which they were broken open as people – to God and to men. I am convinced that just as children and pets are quick to detect whether people fear or like them, so a community of believers knows (often without knowing that it knows!), whether its leader has dared to go on the anvil and has been broken open in this way to God and to man. Without such an encounter we may be able, by natural ability, to lead people to do many things: but we cannot lead them to know or follow God.

The apparently omni-competent leader may well be respected, but will not quickly or easily be loved. Dependence on God is the calling of Christian leadership. Constant drawing attention to ourselves, and baring our soul, is not helpful, but unless we can show our humanity we will be unlikely to lead others well. This involves being able to admit when we have made mistakes and to say so in public, to laugh at ourselves, and to share how we too are on a pilgrimage and have not arrived at the destination. This is particularly true for the preaching ministry. Only as we can share our faltering steps on the journey to wholeness will others feel led by someone who knows what they are going through.

Confidence, loyalty and humanity, however intuitively and subjectively they are experienced, are a trinity of leadership characteristics which are objectively necessary for taking others with us. Confidence is the fruit of our ability to inspire others to see the direction we are taking. Loyalty is the free response of others to come with us on that journey. Humanity is the willingness and ability to be open as a person so that we can 'know and be known' by those who have chosen to follow.

These three aspects of leadership are all included in *love*, for that is the supreme calling and test of leadership: the ability to love a community of people. That capacity to love is the fruit of God's love for us, and should be continually growing to maturity. This means that growth in love is an essential enabler of growth in leadership. How wise of God to structure reality that way!

Understanding the Church
It was John Wimber who introduced me to an analytical tool that has been of great help in understanding another aspect of what goes on when change is taking place in the life of the church or group. It particularly explains why some people just never seem to be with you, while others can seem embarrassingly far ahead of you. It also provides great insight about how to handle these different groups – often all at the same time, as is often necessary.

The key is to realise that within any organisation there are different types and groups of people (illustrated below). They see change, and respond to it, differently. If we can understand what those differences are then we can facilitate rather than frustrate the changes we are seeking to implement.

The picture is of a train with four parts. Out in front is the track-laying vehicle occupied by the *radicals*. They are always keen to find new ways of functioning, and are eager to implement

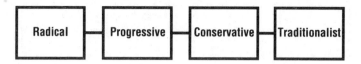

Understanding the church

the vision that is usually very clear to them. Their eyes are on the future and on the way ahead. They are not greatly affected by what is behind them, or by how many are following. These people are usually great disturbers of the peace, yet without their restless and visionary eagerness little advance for the kingdom of God can be made.

The main engine houses the *progressives*. These people have a positive attitude to change, although they are not committed to change for change's sake. They want to weigh the issue carefully before committing themselves: however, they will form the engine of change in any situation. Their ideas often come initially from the radicals, though such ideas will be changed and moderated in the process.

In the carriages sit the *conservatives*, that is those whose attitude to change is more cautious. They expect change to be for the worse, and want to look at it very carefully. They are not opposed, unthinkingly, to all change: but they need persuading. It is the progressives who are best placed to convince the conservatives that change is for the better; the radicals tend to frighten and antagonise them.

Finally, bringing up the rear in the guards van, the *traditionalists* are to be found. They are either looking out of the back of the van seeing how wonderful the place that we came from is, or else they are pulling hard on the brake to reduce speed as much as possible. The theme song of the traditionalists is 'change and decay in all around I see'.

The first time I saw this picture I did an instant action replay of my leadership of the church during the initiation of charismatic renewal, and the work of the building project, and saw what I had intuitively done. I was convinced, from scripture and from experience, that the radicals – or rather the progressives – were right in what they were affirming. Yet I did not want to leave the

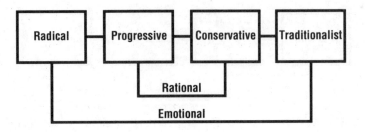

Motivation for change

hesitant and resistant behind. I felt for them in their anxiety, and saw the reasonableness of their arguments. Not dividing the church was second only in importance to moving where the Spirit was leading. This prepared me for receiving the second dimension to this picture.

What was explained was that the radicals and traditionalists are motivated at the *emotional* level. It is ideas that alternately fire and threaten them. By contrast, the progressives and conservatives are motivated at the *rational* level. It is therefore important that we approach these groups in the way that speaks to them. Enthusing the conservatives, or arguing with the traditionalists, is unlikely to yield much fruit.

As I look back at those radicals who have left the church to form a house church, and those traditionalists who have retired to a safer church, I can see how this process has gone on. Rational argument with either group was fruitless.

Two important questions immediately sprang to my mind. First, which is the right group, and second, where is Jesus to be found in this picture?

As far as which group is right, it did not take me long to see that each group is sometimes right as well as sometimes wrong. Obedience involves the willingness both to make radical changes, and to be faithful to the traditions we have inherited. I also saw that any one group, on its own, is unbalanced and wrong. As all members of the one body we really do need each other. In many situations, those who are eager for change have split the track-laying vehicle off from the rest of the train. It certainly makes for faster progress, but can easily end up 'going off the rails', and rarely takes many people along with the vision. Yet those who have sided with the cautious have found that they too have got nowhere, and have often lost many members or failed to win new believers to the faith. Churches which are made up entirely of elderly people have sometimes reached that point by denying the truth, and a place in shaping the church, of those of a more radical and progressive view. Sadly, churches which have chosen that tranquil route find themselves in a siding with no way back.

When I considered the ministry of Jesus I discovered several striking things. The threefold nature of Jesus's ministry fits as the coupling between each of the groups. The *prophetic* element in his preaching, especially about the kingdom and the suffering servant, spoke of the radical changes that God wants to bring about. Such teaching would have found ready support among the radicals and progressives. Yet as a *pastor*, Jesus cared about how people felt, and started from that point. He stood between progressives and conservatives to link them together through his understanding of what each felt. Finally, as *priest* he saw the value of the inheritance of faith and was eager to uphold the truths handed down through the ages.

I also saw that Jesus can be found, at various times, in each camp, yet at the same time seeming to confront that group with the truth that another group was expressing. So, when on the

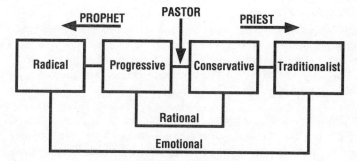

The ministry of Jesus in the process of change

Mount he gathered around him his disciples (the radicals committed to his message) he was at his most traditional. 'Do not think I am come to abolish the Law or prophets, I have not come to abolish but to fulfil them' (Mt 5.17). Conversely, when faced with the traditionalists, the Sanhedrin, he spoke in strongly radical terms, 'Destroy this temple and in three days I will rebuild it.'

Quite intuitively I found myself doing this when we were considering the setting up of the nine o'clock service. It was hardly surprising that 'traditionalists' should be raising all sorts of objections. They were saying something important, and it resulted in our definition of what the leaders of that service had to do about worship. I said, 'You have to do exactly what the rest of the church does – worship God, read and teach from the scriptures, intercede for the church and world, and minister to the people in the power of the Spirit.' We added, 'How you do it – in a way appropriate for those you are seeking to reach – is for you to decide.' In other words, their task was to renew the tradition – not to throw it overboard.

It is so tempting to 'join' the group we emotionally identify with, and then to champion their cause to the point where everyone else is put in the wrong. Yet the fact is that no group can, by itself, build a healthy or balanced church.

The radicals will tell us they know what God wants – they have been on their knees. The conservatives will tell us they can see what needs to happen – they have their feet on the ground. A healthy body can do both, and leadership – like the central nervous system – is the vital communication between the various parts. Without the exercise of unifying leadership the Body of Christ is likely to be spastic in its movements. But it is a costly task because we will always seem to be saying the opposite of what any particular group or person is saying. It is part of what it means for leaders to go the way of the cross. The fact is we do need one another.

The Limits
With this analytical tool, it is possible to see more clearly what is going on, and to find ways of taking the whole church 'in his train' (Is 6.1)! Yet, eager though we should be to include everyone in

the train of events we are about to set in motion, it has to be recognised that there are limits. The painful ministry of Jesus demonstrates this. His primary calling was to do the will of the Father. His leadership ability in handling the whole range of radicals to traditionalists was based on the ultimate expression of love and *humanity*, in which the disciples could have absolute *confidence* and every reason to give unswerving *loyalty*. Yet, when the crunch came, they deserted him. Peter was not able to stay loyal, the rest of the disciples could not take the heat, and Judas turned traitor.

It is all too easy when we struggle as a leader, and are not doing a good job handling others, to project our problems onto others and see everyone who disagrees as a Peter or a Judas. We do need, on the other hand, to recognise that the fact that others are not willing to follow is not necessarily a reflection on us. My experience has taught me to build a small group of people who will support me by helping me to be honest about what is actually happening in such difficult conflict situations. Every leader needs those who can love him or her enough to help us face the truth. When we have faced the obstacles and problems that may be in us, then – with humility but courage – we have to join with Jesus who 'entrusted himself to him who judges justly' (1 Pet 2.23).

Finding Life

Learning to be open to others so that we can give and inspire confidence and loyalty is the fruit not so much of developing new skills in leadership as it is of growing as a person. This happens as we allow God to deal with the blockages to the flow of his love and humanity in us which he desires to give to all, especially those called to leadership.

Understanding and valuing what radicals, progressives, conservatives and traditionalists are saying, and learning where they need to hear what others are saying is the fruit of listening as a person. This has to begin with our listening to God. That listening is not adequate if it is just a rational (analytical) exercise. It involves hearing as a whole person, and includes the intuitive and the spiritual (inspirational) aspects of our humanity.

Here again, growth in leadership arises out of our willingness to allow God to shape us through our experiences of life. Part of this process is learning to get in touch with our emotions and be honest about them; listening to criticism – and affirmation – given to us by others, and being able to discern and distil the truth from both hostility and flattery. As we find life and wholeness and humanity we discover with them the God-given resources to take others with us along the pilgrim way.

Chapter Nine

SOLVING PROBLEMS

At a moving communion service in the old church building, the administration of the elements had just been completed, the worship group had led a time of high praise to God, and I was returning to the communion table to kneel in my accustomed place at the north side of the table. A kneeler enabled the celebrant to be at just the right height to face the service book placed on a stand on the table.

As I slowly – and unthinkingly – lowered myself down I experienced a sinking feeling as my knees went well past their normal resting place. Someone had removed the kneeler! My knees touched the ground a fraction of a second after my chin had made strong and memorable contact with the communion table. Surprise and shock, I am told, were written all over my face.

I looked across the table, with a dazed expression, at my colleague who had been involved in taking the service with me, for sympathy and concern. Instead a broad grin swept across his face. Realising that I had not done any serious injury to myself resulted in his having a scarcely contained fit of giggles. Now we were both incapacitated. Awareness of this fact brought us swiftly back to the job in hand. My colleague leapt to my aid and led the closing prayer so that I had time to compose myself to announce the final hymn and give the blessing.

It was an instructive incident known only to God and us two clergy. It had taken a split second. We had both adapted so fast that no one knew anything of what had happened. Yet learning how to 'keep the show on the road' in the midst of crises, setbacks and problems, large or small, is itself a skill that needs to be learned. All that I have written so far has been about how to discover vision and break out of the endless cycle of activities which all too often takes us nowhere. It has not been about how to keep going, but rather about how to stop and reflect, how consciously to choose a new direction; indeed it has been about how to become pro-active rather than simply re-active.

Yet problems, more serious than the lack of a kneeler, still happen to the best of us. All too often, the table seems to come up and hit us on the chin. The challenge of leadership is therefore to find creative ways in which we can handle that rich mixture of challenge and disaster which life can throw at us. Indeed, skilful leadership can draw potential and positive gain out of impending disaster.

'There are no such things as problems, only opportunities' is a creed I subscribe to more than I am always able to practise, but it is this side of leadership that I want to explore in the remaining chapters. How can we handle the imperfect situations in which all ministry takes place? How can we deal with the organisational tangles we often find ourselves in? Above all, how can we handle ourselves in such a way that we become part of the solutions rather than part of the problems?

Gospel Dynamics
One of the most important lessons I have learned about problem solving came about through the interplay of an *inspirational* insight about Moses, which fed and directed an *intuitive* response to problems.

I had been reading through the life of Moses and meditating on the lessons he had learned in leadership. I reached the point where, after all his hesitations, he agreed to accept the job (was there an alternative – other than death?). Now Moses certainly had a vision – 'bring my people out of Egypt' – but he also had some major problems, chief of which was Pharaoh. However, Pharaoh was not the only problem. Moses did not exactly have a good record in winning the confidence and loyalty of the children of Israel. For him, life had not begun at forty! No wonder he said: 'What if they do not believe me, or listen to me!' (Ex 4.1). That was understandable enough, and has frequently been the plea of leaders down the years. God's answer to Moses was fascinating. He simply said to Moses, 'What is that in your hand?'

> 'A staff,' he replied. The Lord said, 'Throw it on the ground.' Moses threw it on the ground and it became a snake, and he ran from it. The Lord said to him, 'Reach out your hand and take it by the tail.' So Moses reached out and took hold of the snake and it turned back into a staff in his hand. 'This,' said the Lord, 'is so that they may believe that the Lord, the God of their fathers – the God of Abraham, the God of Isaac and the God of Jacob – has appeared to you.'
>
> (Ex 4.2–5)

Moses was to begin with what was in his hand. And a very good place to begin too! I considered what was in my hand – a whole series of pressing problems. I would love to have thrown them to the ground! The building needed considerable attention, we were short of cash, there was conflict in the church, and so on. That was just where God called Moses to begin: with what was in his hand.

When Moses took authority over what was in his hand he found God was at work, and that his ministry, calling and authority were authenticated both to Israel and to Pharaoh, out of that action. In a moment of insight (*inspiration*) I saw that the pressing problems were not an obstacle to the fulfilment of the vision, but God's appointed means. His call to me was to take authority over them.

Pressing Problems

Later on this insight crystallised for me into *applying gospel principles to pressing problems*. I had already been doing this, but the insight helped me to see the significance of my *intuitive* response to the situation, and encouraged me to see the value of what I was doing. No longer did I need to say, in the face of endless problems and frustrations, 'If only we did not have all these problems we could get on with the real job.' I now saw that the difficulties we faced were the *real* job; the opportunity to demonstrate God's power and mercy to redeem his people when they are faced with the petty frustrations, failures and fears that so often form the chief obstacles to growth. Moreover it was also God's way of preparing the church for the implementation of the vision we had. Having seen him at work in the practical details of the life of the church we would be better placed to trust him with some of the bigger challenges which were ahead.

Applying gospel dynamics to pressing problems is a key way into implementing vision. It is how we gain the confidence of the church sufficiently to lead it into greater ventures. If we can be trusted to lead the church through pressing practical problems we will have gained a body of people who will follow us into the more important realms of faith, worship, witness, and the releasing of the power of God in the local community.

For example, if the church is facing a financial problem, that is where we are to begin. Viewed from one side it is a problem; viewed from the other it is both an opportunity and a challenge. We can call the church to prayer, to faithful trusting of God for the situation, to sacrificial giving, and see what God will do.

In the first church I had responsibility for, there was urgent need for one hundred pounds to buy chairs for the congregation. Even in the late sixties one hundred pounds did not buy many chairs, but we did not have many people to sit on them! The idea of prayer, faith, and sacrifice did not come easily. The church went along with the new curate-in-charge and his crazy ideas about trusting God. They were willing to indulge my whims a little in the early days of my ministry. Then it dawned on people that I had no plans for any fund-raising events of any sort. With only three weeks to go they realised to their horror that all I had planned was a gift day: yet one hundred pounds was more than the total income of the church in the previous year. 'Somebody must *do* something,' was the reaction of the church committee. They decided they had to organise a fund-raising event, so they came to me to get my agreement to a concert on the Saturday evening before the gift day.

My first reaction was to stand firm, explain about trusting God and giving sacrificially, and to say that such an event would be a denial of faith. Then in a moment of insight from God I saw that this whole venture was being run on *my* faith not theirs. It was as though God was telling me to take the attitude of 'have this one on me'.

On the night before the gift day we had a concert. It was a happy and successful occasion – except for just one thing. When all the counting was done the balance of income over expenditure was seventeen shillings and sixpence (85p). The next day I was able to announce that we were now only needing £99 2s. 6d! We experienced God's faithfulness to us by giving us over one hundred pounds that day. Out of that experience many were renewed in faith; others began to see and trust God for the first time or in a new and more immediate way. When greater tests subsequently stood before us we were already a church that had experienced God's provision in the context of prayer and sacrifice – we already had a track record.

Our financial problem had been redeemed. Not only did we have the money we needed, but we were richer in other ways; richer in faith, in sacrifice, and in the sense of being bound together in a fellowship on the move. Gospel dynamics were bearing fruit.

Even more important than the financial area is the realm of personal relationships, so often a minefield in the life of a church. Our commission as Christians is to be ministers of reconciliation. It is right at the heart of God's purposes in Christ and his work on the cross. The history of the divisions of the Christian church is a sad commentary on our inability to live by our message. Yet neither the local, national, nor worldwide church, can make much impact until it begins to *live* the gospel. Thus the facing, and tackling, of relationship problems is not just to be undertaken when, in the last analysis, they cannot be suppressed any longer. Reconciliation is the essence of the gospel, and the problems in relationships are the opportunity for demonstrating the power of the gospel in the here and now.

The apostle Paul talks about the church being a colony of heaven, the outpost of a different way of living. In honesty, this different way of relating has, in our experience, been most put to the test at moments of greatest change. For example, moving into the charismatic dimension brought a host of tensions. Yet it was at just that point that we learned to respect each other, to listen to what the other was saying, and to hold on in love even where we disagreed.

From finances to personal relationships, the applying of gospel principles to pressing problems will leave us richer as a church, and more prepared for the greater tasks he has called us to.

However, God's concern is not simply with where we get to, but with how we travel.

I have repeatedly seen the relevance of this truth as I have watched newly appointed leaders enthusiastically tackle their new task. They want to get on with what they see as 'the real job' – to change the agenda of the church. Sometimes that is just what they are called to do. But more often it is the tackling of existing problems that is God's way through to the implementing of the vision they have. The new leader, whether of a fellowship group, or youth work, or of a church needs to see the pressing problems with the eye of faith. That way we walk right into God's strategy for our leadership of others.

Certainly, arriving at St Thomas's and finding it geared for a building project, I did not sense God's leading in that direction. I deliberately stalled on that issue and changed the agenda. However, there were other pressing problems, including the re-ordering of the patterns of worship and the opening up of the fortress-like churchyard, which we did tackle. We faced them with faith, and met with God through applying gospel principles to them. They thus became for us, at that moment in our development, 'the real job' God was calling us to tackle. Had we avoided them by focusing on a much greater vision, we would never have been prepared for what lay ahead.

Variety is the Spice of Life
Many problems have faced us on the journey from a church of two hundred to one where over a thousand people worship together every week. Although the problems have seemed to be endless, and many of them unique to our particular circumstances, they have fallen nonetheless into three broad categories which have universal relevance. This categorising of problems has become an important part in the process of finding solutions. Once the nature of the problem is defined, then it is that much clearer how gospel principles can be applied.

Out of our teamwork as a staff, we developed an *analytical* tool in the form of a framework within which to understand the nature of the problems we have been facing.

First are the functional problems. We have faced problems about the unsuitability of our buildings, and about our lack of money. We have had to cope with organising a large group of people. We have faced problems of communication and have alternately been accused of being secretive, or wasting paper. We have faced the practical problems associated with organising a multitude of activities (often over twelve a day, every day of the week). We have found that deeper issues can lurk behind what at first sight just seems to be a functional problem, and often explain the strength of reaction that can result from what seems to be a very straightforward change.

Second are the emotional barriers. I now see the emotional barriers to change as the most crucial to be faced and overcome. I have already told how, during the time of initial charismatic renewal, I intuitively sided with those who were working for change and renewal while seeking to take the whole church along at the same time. I was operating as a progressive. Ever since that time the church has continued to be open to change, though it is an attitude that has only been built slowly, and not without the cost of going through major emotional barriers.

It was at that time, and quite specifically because of our experience of renewal, that a close-knit group of fifty people from one Christian organisation left the church – all on one day. Growth often begins with decline, as Gideon experienced. The emotional cost of facing such decline is indeed high. The 'remnant' theology of the Old Testament points to decline down to just a small group, called to such a quality of obedience that God can rebuild the whole nation through it. Jesus is the supreme remnant and in his own ministry saw decline to the point where only one or two women were with him right through to the cross, before the seed died and a vast harvest was reaped of which the church today is a part. This is not to justify all decline as such. But the securing of worthwhile change and growth often first involves loss and decline, which feels costly and from which people seek to protect themselves.

A simple graph has expressed this pattern, which has been repeated in many areas of the life of the church. Previously used in connection with delegation, it applies also to church growth.

The diagram, which plots effectiveness against time, shows that change is likely to have an initially negative effect. Only after some time has elapsed do the benefits of change emerge. This

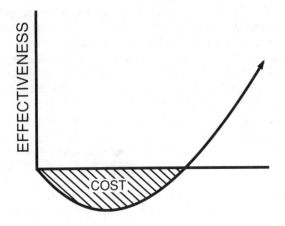

Decline and growth through the impact of change

makes leadership of change a costly business. It involves risk and faith, for the first results are often negative. Only by holding on can we reap the fruits.

I have seen this pattern being repeated so often that I am now convinced that no man can be a facilitator of growth who cannot first handle decline. This is often one of those points at which God takes a leader onto the anvil of painful experience in which we have to let go of hopes, success and reputation and hold onto him alone. It was part of what God was doing in calling Abraham to sacrifice Isaac. We tend to read that incident in terms of what God was wanting to take from Abraham, yet the truth is that God's purpose was to give him a closer understanding of the Father-heart of God (who was actually to give *his* only son), and to cause Abraham to be bonded to the Giver more profoundly than to the gift (Isaac).

The pattern of 'through the cross to resurrection life' underlies this difficult journey. It is a costly emotional path for a church and for a leader to have to walk, but it is the way that leads to life. Growth, in all areas of life, has to do with openness, faith and generosity. If we hold on tightly to what we have, and are unwilling to risk trouble, we will lose even what we have. Only the open hand that can let people go, and can also receive the pain of rejection (the imprint of the nails), is in a place to receive the resurrection life that God desires to give.

I was discussing recently with a group of Scandinavian pastors a problem that their charismatic churches have not overcome in nearly twenty years of renewal. They have not seen any significant growth. As we talked it began to dawn on me that 'holding everyone together' was a very high value in their situation. So was the price – thousands were effectively being kept from hearing the gospel. I drew the effectiveness/time graph and shaded in the initial debit area and asked if anyone had dared enter that area. It was a holy moment. This fine group of pastors knew the cost of such a question, and that one of them might well have to be the first to go this way. I could promise no easy ride, but I believe they caught a vision of what God could do if he found one willing to co-operate with his costly way of bringing growth to his church. A moment of revelation, divine inspiration, was happening before my eyes, and a crucial emotional barrier was being faced.

Third are the spiritual obstacles. Though renewal has released a well-spring of spiritual life in the church, it did not solve all our problems. The renewal has needed renewing, just as the Reformation needs continually to be reformed. D. L. Moody, the great nineteenth century evangelist, when asked if he was filled with the Spirit said, 'Yes, but I leak!' That has been our experience, and we have had to admit it. Probably the major spiritual problem that we have faced as a church was what I now call 'post-project depression'. Elijah is a clear example of a man who suffered an emotional and spiritual reaction to a major 'success' in God's service. Our spiritual malaise was very slow growing. We seemed to ride the initial trials well. Three years after the building project the church was growing faster than at any time in the previous twenty years. We appeared to have weathered any post-project blues. But that was not to be the case.

Central to our struggles was the lack of focus to our vision. The building project had been such a concrete goal. Everyone could see if it was working or not. Everyone could see and rejoice at its completion. Yet when we came to look for the vision which lay beyond the re-building, the medium we were working with seemed to change from concrete to mist. We had said our real goal was not just to build a new building; it was and is to build the kingdom. But what is the kingdom? How can you define it without perverting it? If you cannot define the goal then how can you tell whether you are making any progress towards its attainment or not?

It has taken a further breaking in of God's Spirit, much prayer, and thorough analysis of our situation to find the way through this malaise. Intuition, inspiration, and analysis have been closely interwoven in the way we have discovered answers to these varied problems and obstacles in our walk with God. Distinguishing the underlying spiritual issue from its overlay of emotional and functional issues was the vital first step.

The value of this three-fold framework of the spiritual, emotional and functional aspects of any problem was well illustrated in a recent meeting with the fellowship group leaders of one of our congregations. We were addressing the matter of evangelism through our supporting fellowships.

I had used the working model I have of Lewin's force field theory to introduce the question I was wanting us to face: 'What are the constraints to sharing our faith with others?' After a positive time of sharing how some within our groups were being effective in leading others to faith, we attempted to identify the obstacles to greater effectiveness. A number of problems were identified. People were too busy to have many non-Christian friends. Having separate fellowship groups for each congregation meant that the membership of each group tended to live further away from each other than before: this led to lack of contact with neighbours.

At that point in the meeting I sensed that the leaders were saying 'that is it'. However, I instinctively felt uncomfortable. The problem was not so easily 'bottomed'. In that moment of hesitation I realised that all the problems we had identified were at the *functional* level. We had not touched on the *emotional* barriers (embarrassment in speaking about God), or the *spiritual* barriers (lack of a living experience of God to express): yet these were the crucial problems. Once we began to face these we moved into a new dimension of openness and honesty about ourselves and our emotions. We saw also our need of God and were driven to prayer to seek his grace for the work he had called us to. That step brought us into living touch with him – which is what the problem at heart was all about.

This story also illustrates the full value of this analytical tool. It not only enabled us to discover what the problem really was, and therefore to apply an appropriate solution, it also helped us to see that some problems, maybe most, actually come to us in layers. They have a functional, an emotional, and a spiritual dimension to them. It is important to discern this and therefore to apply the appropriate solution to each component. In the incident above we talked about the functional problems, we faced the emotional problems by owning them and being open with one another, and we faced the spiritual dimension by admitting it to each other, and then by turning to God in prayer.

If gospel dynamics are to be applied successfully to pressing problems then it is important for us to pay attention to the layers within them. Not only does each need dealing with, but each is also God's opportunity to incarnate his truth in the leader and the group or church.

Getting it Wrong

All that I have written so far about facing problems has implied that what is being faced are inherited problems. However, there is another, potentially more difficult, type of problem to solve: the ones we have brought upon ourselves. The longer we are in one church, the more this is likely to be the case. Yet it is most difficult to admit them. It is not something that secular leadership practises much, but can be a life-giving mark of leadership in the kingdom of God, and is often the starting point for resolving such problems. To admit mistakes is rarely harmful. Everybody else knows it – and has been talking about it for ages! If the leader (or leadership) can admit when they have been wrong they will be trusted more genuinely at other times. People will know that they do not have to go through the charade of the emperor's new clothes about the vicar's latest ideas.

I want, therefore, to draw out the fundamental lessons from the mistakes to which I have been a party: the problems I have been responsible for creating – and subsequently having to solve too. I have referred to these problems already, but I now want to share the lessons I have learned from my own mistakes. In doing so I hope to encourage others to dare to own their mistakes, to correct them and to learn from them. It is not easy, but it is part of what it means to be called to share in God's work of redeeming this fallen world. It is one of the ways in which we meet God – in this painful place of weakness.

We called our building project the Church Extension Project in order to express the double meaning of extending the buildings, and also of being extended in God's service as a church. At one point we decided to express that commitment to the extension of the church fellowship by saying that we were seeking to 'double the number of believers within the next three years'. It did not work out. First, we were too busy getting the building altered to give proper attention to evangelism. Second, we had not done our analytical homework so we had no way of measuring the number of people coming to faith. We realised that we could double the membership of the church by Christians moving in from other areas without actually bringing one person to faith.

In the early eighties we completely re-structured our fellowship groups, supposedly to release more people for service in the local community. However, we were not functioning properly under the call of God in this and found, to our surprise, that if all you are doing is re-ordering something, then all that will change are the structures. Inspiration was lacking.

In the mid-eighties we ran into a major problem time in the leadership (which I have outlined in *In the Crucible*). Several people saw the problems well ahead of time, but my ears were closed to what my intuition was telling me. The failure to listen to them, or even to allow my own instincts to have voice, resulted in much pain and struggle. If only I had listened to my feelings, I have subsequently thought, how different things would have been.

Personal Learning
The connecting thread between those three incidents of failure was that at least one of the elements from the framework of learning was missing in each situation. We had not done our homework on how we would *analyse* our growth to be effective. Our organisational changes lacked an underlying spiritual *in-*

spiration: and we failed to listen to the *intuition* of several who were close to the leadership when we hit problems. Making mistakes has therefore served to underline the validity of the framework for learning. This is redemption in action. God is able to take our mistakes and turn them into blessing, unity, a greater dependence on him, and growth: as long as we will have the honesty to admit them and the faith to seek his help in resolving them.

Facing problems, both the ones inherent in the situation and also the ones of my own making, has also underlined to me the fact that learning takes place most effectively at the place of weakness, where the One who redeems is able to turn failure into fruitfulness. This learning can only happen if we are able to listen to what God is saying through 'the blessed sacrament of the present moment'. It grows out of an openness of relationship to God in which repentance and faith are a constant dynamic. Being able to own the truth before God is an expression of the honesty which is essential to this learning. The skill of solving problems is therefore truly rooted in the security of our relationship to God, while hiding from him will inevitably cause us to hide from others as Adam and Eve did in the garden – by blame-shifting in one form or another.

Paradoxically, it is seeming success and a smooth-running operation which most easily immunise us from this vital learning process. Needing to see only the good news of our situation, and to fail to face the weaknesses, is what most easily frustrates this learning process. Morton Kelsey, in *The Other Side of Silence*, expresses this fact about learning in the place of weakness:

> An efficient busy life, which keeps us occupied without being harried and keeps our attention entirely on interesting outer things, is probably more potentially destructive of spiritual growth than debauchery or alcohol or hard drugs. These obvious indulgences usually at least lead to emptiness, and sometimes to despair, and in such times one is dangerously vulnerable to being found by God. On the other hand, a quiet, efficient and busy life spent continuously in good works can shield an individual most effectively from any plunge into the depth where God dwells.

It is in the depths, the places of weakness, failure and despair, that God delights to break in. Problem solving can therefore be welcomed for what it is – perhaps the greatest opportunity for learning leadership through experience. All we need is the courage and faith to own the problems!

Chapter Ten

STRUCTURING FOR GROWTH

Faced with a two-year gap between leaving school and having a place at university, I had to decide how best to make use of that period. National service was due to come to an end during my university course so I could have avoided it. Yet if, as was possible, it had been extended, I would have been faced with two years' national service after university. I decided to opt for an early call-up.

Having had a boarding school education I could see that such experience would be a great help in equipping me to know and work with people with a different background from my own. I ended up in a Royal Artillery regiment which became the first unit of the army to receive guided missiles: not the most obvious preparation for someone seeking to be ordained! However, I thoroughly enjoyed the experience of working with a very mixed group of people. I was just getting into my stride when the commanding officer called me in and told me I was to become the assistant adjutant. The adjutant was the man who ran, or managed, the whole operation. What I discovered was that he was away most of the time, skiing for the army, so – as the scriptures put it – 'the lot fell on' me. I felt both daunted at the responsibility and frustrated that the relationships I had just begun to establish were being removed at a stroke. I had been shunted into a siding, and I could not see God in the situation. Yet it was indeed his doing, and proved to be part of his action (inspiration) to prepare me for what lay ahead. This was to be my initiation into the art of learning leadership through experience, focusing on one facet that would be essential to me in the future.

Over the remaining nine months I was introduced into a new world of files, pending trays, rotas and returns, accident claim forms and situation papers. I ended up learning much and loving the job. The experience helped me not to be afraid of paper work, and taught me both how to operate a filing system, and just how much hidden work goes on to make something like a regiment (or a church) run smoothly.

This experience was reinforced by working with two vicars, Michael Baughen in Manchester and Dick Sargent in Wolverhampton, who were both well organised men. They needed to be. Michael was not only handling a growing church, developing a city-wide evangelical witness, and launching a building project, but also writing, editing and launching *Youth Praise*. Dick Sargent was handling a parish of over forty thousand people, with three worship centres, where we regularly had eight weddings a Saturday throughout the summer, and over sixty funerals a month in the winter. I learned much from them both, as clearly God intended I should.

The Gift of Administration
Perhaps the most important lesson was that administration is a healthy and wholesome part of Christian ministry. It is this subject of planning, organisation and management which I now want to address. As with problem solving, which was considered in the last chapter, unless we become proficient in this area then the implementing of vision, however great and authentic, will always turn out to be stunted. Management cannot of itself bring in the kingdom, but I have learned that it is vital if the work of the kingdom is to have room to grow and advance.

This positive attitude to planning and organisation was something I needed as an anchor when my experience of the Holy Spirit led me into the world of the charismatic movement. There I frequently came across a sacred/secular divide which labels some things 'spiritual' and of great importance, and relegates other things as 'practical' (or lower still, 'administration') and consequently of little importance. Not that this was ever voiced or spelt out, but it was part of the atmosphere and the unconscious assumptions. I caught glimpses of it from time to time when I heard people say, 'We are not going to organise anything, we are going to trust God,' and when I heard the hushed reverence with which preachers were listened to who began by saying they had not prepared but had 'just left it to the Holy Spirit'; though I did detect a restlessness in the congregation as time went on, and the preacher went round and round his subject.

Naturally, in seeking to handle and interpret my experience of the Holy Spirit, I turned to Paul's letters to the Corinthians – especially to 1 Corinthians 12–14.

It was there, in among the new gifts I was seeing around me – tongues, interpretation, healing, words of knowledge, prophecy – that I discovered that Paul had slipped a joker into the pack: 'the gift of administration'. I was relieved to see that at least the apostle had his feet on the ground. This was further reinforced for me by his repeated use of the phrase 'let everything be done decently and in order', which comes like a sudden Anglican thunderbolt out of a clear blue Pentecostal sky.

It so happened that the church, at just that time, had made a first attempt at harnessing the gifts of the whole church membership through what we called 'a gifts gift day'. In preparation for this we had been drawing to the church's attention a number of Old Testament scriptures. Moses had a highly organised plan – from God – for the building of the temple. He also relied upon the Holy Spirit to inspire the craftsmen to do the work. There was no dichotomy in his mind between the sacred and secular. He would not have been able to understand the terms. David, that amazingly creative musician, knew how to organise a thing or two. He set up superb structures for his army, created a job akin to a chancellor of the exchequer, and arranged a complex rota system for priests and singers. In such scriptures as these I was seeing the integration of openness to God and the freedom of the Spirit, with a well ordered operation and good organisation.

Super-spirituality

The inspiration of God through my experience of life, and out of the scriptures, had equipped me to have a positive attitude to planning, organisation and management for which I remain

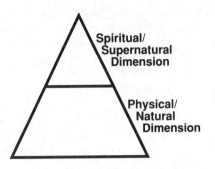

The super-spirituality triangle

deeply grateful. Indeed without it, I would have been unable to become involved in the structuring for growth which has been so essential in enabling St Thomas's to keep moving through the various phases of its development.

However, belittling remarks about administration continue to be a part of my experience. It provoked me at one stage to try to understand why this was so. Out of the blue, in a moment of intuition, a diagram came to mind. It interpreted my experience and gave a vital insight about the importance of getting the structures right if the Spirit is to have the freedom to move that God intends. The picture is of a triangle, which I call the 'super-spirituality triangle':

The triangle represents life as God created it to be. The top

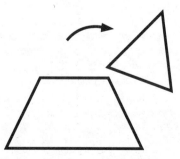

The impact of the Fall on man's experience of reality

half represents the spiritual dimension that God brings back into a believer's life through faith in Christ (redemption). The base of the triangle represents the practical and physical dimension of human existence (creation). At the Fall these two parts became broken and separate.

The triangle helps us understand various situations, such as what happens when a Christian says to a non-Christian (pointing to the top half of the triangle): 'Your life is base – it has no point: we have found the point to life!' Often the non-Christian looks at the life the Christian has and (pointing to the bottom half of the triangle) says 'Yes, but there seems to be more to my life than yours – I'm not changing!'

It shows more than this however. The Fall of man has affected the whole of human existence. This is what the Puritan teachers meant when they spoke about 'total depravity'. They were not saying that man was as bad as he could be, but simply that every area of his life was marred by that break in relationship with God. The Fall has broken not only our spiritual nature but also our practical ability to order our world. The troubled state of the world's environment is tragic yet eloquent testimony to this fact.

The good news is that both are redeemed by Christ. When the triangle is put back together it demonstrates how the spiritual can inform and infuse the physical, yet also be upheld and sustained by the practical, such as our planning and organisation. The church should be the place where the world can see a redeemed organisation.

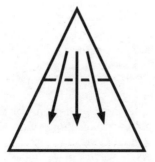

Creation redeemed

Thus the person who can seem 'super-spiritual', often being marked by intensity and a hot-house approach to knowing God, but who is not integrated well with their humanity, is not the picture of creation redeemed that they first appear to be. In Christian service they often function like super-nova stars, shining with great brilliance for a while and drawing everyone's attention to their endeavours, but not for long. Soon the brilliance has gone, and the star is nowhere to be seen. Often the steady plodders are left to pick up the pieces. Such stars have their value of course. Bright stars help us to get our bearings and can show us the way. They are radicals (though let me hasten to add that not all radicals are super-spiritual). However, unless they are well harnessed to progressives and conservatives, they will not mature as people and their work will not last. That harnessing is one of the best ways of helping such people towards personal growth: just as their presence in a group can draw out a conservative person's dormant radical and spiritual aspects.

The same dynamic can happen with a church. To be full of spiritual vitality is great, but if it is not well integrated with the human and practical aspects of life, it will fail to proclaim the wholeness of the gospel and will end up being stunted in its growth. Which is why we need to learn how to handle the practical aspects of ordering the life of a church.

Ordering the Renewal
With this perspective we were well placed, by the providence of God, not to fall into the trap of thinking that planning and good order are alternative, or hostile, to the free moving of the Holy Spirit. Tom Smail came to us one Sunday and simply 'rejoiced to see your good order', having come from a situation where 'the freedom of the Spirit' was an excuse for a complete lack of planning and preparation. He commented that his experience was that the Holy Spirit seemed to work with greater freedom when man had properly prepared for the practical arrangements. That encouragement set us firmly on the path of seeking a well-ordered experience of renewal, which would truly exemplify creation redeemed.

There are dangers, however, in seeking good order. Indeed we have known times when we have quenched the Spirit by over-planning as much as would have happened by not planning. We are not the first of God's people to encounter the problem – for example, on one occasion King David was wrong to count the people, despite his calling to administer their life. Nonetheless, the dangers of over-planning are no more of an argument for not planning than over-eating is an argument for starving to death. The right response to abuse is not disuse but proper use, by seeking to learn through our experience in this area.

We had come to value what are sometimes called 'enabling structures': ways of operating that make it easier and more likely that we will do what we are wanting to do. There are two illustrations of this.

The first is our Commitment Sunday pattern for the church's giving, which involves everyone completing a card at the end of the year to say how much they will be giving in the coming year. It is a very simple annual practice, yet one which has been a major factor in providing the level of giving needed to sustain the work.

Second, when we sensed God calling us to be a more loving church, we preached on the theme for several months – without any great evidence of change. However, when we developed supporting fellowships, small home groups in which we could practise the preaching, things rapidly began to change.

These two simple examples demonstrate a principle that has come to the fore again and again over the years – if growth is to occur, there have to be structures for it. Though we cannot programme growth, it is our responsibility as leaders, as much as any other spiritual responsibility, to plan and prepare for it.

New Wineskins

From those early days of renewal we were enabled to sustain growth because we had paid attention to structures at every level of the church's life. In that time some solid work was done on setting up structures that would help the growth of the church. Several principles began to emerge.

First we realised that we needed elastic structures. If growth was to be sustained, we needed to ask not only whether the structures we set up would work now, but whether they would work when the church was half as big again. We had seen this to be essential for our supporting fellowships. They were established on a 'growth by division' principle so that when they reached sixteen or so members the group divided into two. In that way our initial three groups became, within four years, fifteen groups. After a further four years we had over thirty of them. We recently passed the sixty mark. Equally, in more recent times, in establishing our (at present) four congregations, we have been looking to the future and seeing how this structure is elastic and will enable us to add further congregations in due course.

Second we wanted to have flexible structures. The church lives within a changing environment and it is important that it is able to adapt to it speedily. We wanted to find a way of organising ourselves that could quickly be adapted to changing circumstances. We were able to do this with lay leadership when the massive demands of the building project came on us. The person handling the finances of that project delegated a very considerable amount of work on the regular income and accounts to others. Equally, the organisation of the Sunday services needed to be taken over by others so that churchwardens could shoulder the work of the building project. We appointed deputy wardens to handle stewarding and the routine fabric work of the church. Equally, when – in changed circumstances – we no longer needed that sort of help, we simply dropped the role of deputy warden.

Third we went for purposeful structures. We had our eye all the time on what the task or goal was that we were seeking to achieve. We then designed structures to fit that goal. The value of the structure lay only in how far it helped us to achieve our goals. If it was an inefficient tool we changed it, if it was ineffective we scrapped it. We sought never to let the structure dictate the task, but rather the task to define what structure we needed.

This has led us into continual review of what we were doing, why we were doing it, and whether the present way was the best or not.

Typical of this was our review of our parish magazine format. Initially I had simply sought an updating of its layout. However, once we began to look at it those who were helping in the review started to ask all sorts of questions, the most important being, 'Who is it aimed at?' We quickly realised that two different groups were being addressed. One was the parish population, the other was the church membership. They needed different information and a different form of communication. Out of that emerged the plan to have a monthly internal newsheet, and a termly parish newsheet. We were not afraid to scrap outdated institutions, such as the parish *Messenger* and its delivery rounds, once we saw a better way of achieving our purpose than the existing arrangement. That has been a constant mark of how we have sought to work.

Developing Good Structures
With only a limited number of other parish churches travelling the same journey, much of what we have learned has had to be through simply being on the anvil, believing God for his continued shaping and re-shaping of us. Our task has nonetheless been to accept the spiritual responsibility he has given us to keep reviewing the effectiveness of what we are doing. To this end we have come to take four particular steps in managing the way we work as a church.

The first and most important step has been continually to adapt the structures to fulfil the task. This has meant changing how we operate, as we have grown. It means that nothing is immune from change. The goal is to grow, and the question about all our leadership structures is simply whether it helps or hinders that growth. If it hinders, it needs to go. The structures must fit the task, not the task fit the structures.

The second step has been to work in small teams. We learnt the value of this in the building project when three, then four, of us handled the whole venture. We have implemented the same style with our committees. We avoid the label 'committee' wherever possible, and talk rather about teams, such as the fabric team and the finance team. This is expressing an important principle and practice. All such teams are given full responsibility to get on and do the job. To that end they are given the resources and the authority they need. At present the fabric team is allocated a budget of over ten thousand pounds a year to care for all the buildings we own. Once a year it reports to the church council on its priorities for the coming year. At the end of the year it reports back. In the final issue the church council has the responsibility, but it is fully delegated to the fabric team. Unless there is need of some major capital item beyond the budget, the church council discusses fabric only once a year, other than to receive reports.

I am convinced that the structures of the church, along with the rest of its life, need to show evidence of redemption. So much of modern democratic society is a form of institutionalised distrust.

We have sought to build structures of trust, and accountability, and to enable decisions to be made speedily. Recently we have given the leaders of these teams authority to act on behalf of the teams without calling a meeting. If some decision is needed it is therefore possible to get the leaders of several teams together within the week and make the decision, thus cutting through the process of referring items from one committee's monthly meeting to another committee's monthly meeting, and back again round the bureaucratic spiral.

The third step has been to separate the pastoral and eldership roles. As I watched other churches set up elderships I found myself unconvinced about what was being done. The number of elders needed to pastor a church invariably meant a large unwieldy team that was inefficient at decision making. We have over fifteen pastoral leaders and are continually adding to that number. The pastoral care of the church needs their full attention, and we have not distracted them with other responsibilities.

The fourth step has been to integrate the spiritual and institutional aspects of the church's life. We have done this by exercising a form of eldership with the two Anglican church wardens and the Baptist church secretary (who, for the sake of simplicity is now called the Baptist warden). This has been possible because of an agreement with the whole church to put the emphasis on appointing, rather than electing, people to these positions. These three people function in an advisory role to the vicar, Baptist minister, and the whole staff team (six, at present). We have been enormously blessed by a series of very fine wardens who act as a conduit for the concerns of the congregation, enable all of us in full-time ministry to be accountable to others, and continually give wise advice and incisive comments on how the staff team is functioning. They are a godsend, a life-line, and – on occasions – an awesome trio!

Crisis Points

The story I have told thus far of how, and why, structures which facilitated growth have been developed has not greatly separated out the elements of inspiration, intuition and analysis. That is part of the story. Nowhere have I been more aware of this trinity of concerns being woven together in almost inseparable union. But this is not the whole story.

It would have been so much easier if the growth of the church had been like the dotted line on the graph below, a steady and increasing progression. I have to report that life, for us, has not been like that. The solid line has been more the description of the growth we have experienced. Times of growth have repeatedly not been sustained. We have reached a plateau, and then we have had to confront the problems which have created a barrier to further growth. Once having discovered and released the constraints and made the changes necessary, we have been able to move on to further growth – only to find that we have reached another plateau, and that the whole exercise has to be repeated. This is the other half of the story: our structuring for growth has had to include those moments of major readjustment in the whole way that the church is working in order to break through

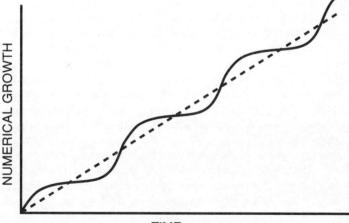

The pattern of growth of the church

the plateaux. Each time the problems, and solutions, have been unique.

Three such crisis points stand out for me. They were crisis points not so much in terms of terrible problems threatening the unity of the church, but in the true sense of vital moments of choice. We could either settle for what we had, or make major choices and changes – with all that that would involve – to release further growth.

The first such decision was when we hit the problems associated with reaching the two hundred membership level. One of the problems was the strain on the pastoral care of the church. I felt overstretched, and the church felt less cared for. Another problem was the increasing insufficiency of the informal way of relying largely on word of mouth to pass on ideas and information. Now people were feeling left out. We had assumed that people knew each other well enough to be able to spot the newcomer, but that was becoming less and less true.

The second crisis was when we reached the 'full church' point. I had already seen that this was the point to which most churches grow – and then stop. Ahead of this dangerous point I had enunciated the principle that 'our goal is not so much to fill the church with believers as to empty the surrounding community of unbelievers'. That immediately meant that we needed to think in terms of thousands coming to faith, rather than just hundreds. The greatest problem associated with this particular plateau is that it is such a happy state to be in! It feels good to be full. But nature warns us that for living things to be full, whether the seed or the egg, one of two things must happen. Either a new form of life will be born – through what feels like death – or there will be still-birth. You cannot have a healthy state of fullness which remains that way.

The third such crisis point has been the most subtle and elusive. It has to do with the process of becoming a large church. Only now can I understand what the church growth experts mean when they say that 'a large church is not just a big form of a small church; it is a different animal'. For us there has had to be a painful process of metamorphosis from one state to another. After three years, we think we may be through that process, but whether the fruit of further significant growth will result remains to be seen in the coming years.

Repeated Pattern
In each of these plateau phases I can now see a repeated pattern of how the problem has been identified and dealt with, again involving intuition, analysis and inspiration.

The first stage has always been an intuitive one. Significantly, it is not primarily through monitoring attendances at services, but through a growing feeling of loss of fulfilment, effectiveness and joy. It is so easy to deny these feelings, and I have often done so. Yet that only means that we meet the problem again in due course, in a more virulent form. When we were at the two hundred barrier I was feeling a failure as a pastor, knowing people less well, and the church mirrored that by feeling less part of what was going on. Our attention shifted from being focused out in love and care to those around, to looking inwards at how we were feeling. When the 'church full' plateau was reached it was a feeling of bureaucracy which was most evident.

With six hundred or so people it was no longer possible through personal relationships to recruit people known to be effective in children's work. The leader of the children's work could not possibly know who might be gifted in that way: so a letter had to be sent to fellowship group leaders asking them to fill in the tear-off slip with names of those they thought might be appropriate. Yet we seem to have a church (like all the others?) which has an allergy to filling in forms!

The evidence that we had reached (at least by British standards) the so-called 'large church' plateau emerged as the structures we had set up so carefully to facilitate growth had imperceptibly become so complex and interwoven that it was difficult for anyone to know how the whole operation worked and who was responsible for what. New staff and new members had difficulty understanding how the church operated, and I seemed trapped as the one common factor essential to every operation. It was both exhausting and frustrating – and not very productive.

The second stage in dealing with the plateau has been in each case an analytical one. We read about church growth theory on the two hundred barrier and how to overcome it. We looked

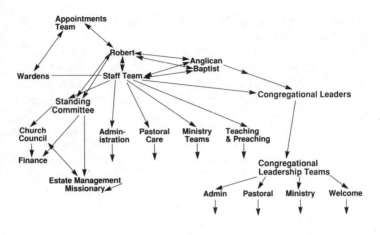

The organisational structure which, like Topsy, 'just grewed'

around at other churches and how they were dealing with growing through the church-full phase. We analysed our management structures to see if they were suited to the large church phase into which we sensed we were moving. To this end one of our churchwardens attempted to draw an organisational chart of how we operated. It looked for all the world like a disorganisation chart. I christened it the Tanglewood secrets! It is reproduced above as a warning, not a pattern to be copied.

The third stage has been the inspirational one. Each time we have discovered some word, insight or act of God which has brought us through to a new stage of growth. Yes, there have had to be structural changes each time as well, but in the final issue it has been a new stage in the life of the church, initiated by God, which has taken us into the new phase of growth. He has certainly honoured our commitment to structuring for growth.

Renewal, which threatened in the first stages to empty the church, was the rekindling of faith which caused the church to proclaim the gospel with a new sense of immediacy and conviction, leading to many being added to the church, and taking us through the two hundred barrier. The 'church full' phase was broken through almost before we had identified the problem by the sovereign act of God in bringing about the establishing of the nine o'clock service – and its subsequent effect of causing us to move into 'congregations'.

In the most recent plateau we have only begun to see part of that divine renewal which I now come to expect; but what we have seen is significant in itself and worth reporting.

Untangling the Tangle

'It happened in this wise.' Having identified the 'Tanglewood secrets' nature of our leadership structures we brought together a group of fifty senior leaders in the church (including the staff team and church council) and shared with them the problem. This was before we saw any answers. We wanted them to know how we saw the situation, we wanted to hear how they saw the problem and we wanted to pray together. After we set out the problem and listened to much wise counsel, we turned to prayer. In the midst of that prayer one of the members of the group, who was among the least interested in a debate on organisational structures, shared a picture. It was of a child's spirograph design produced by interlocking circles. She said she did not know what it meant, but thought it had to do with teams of leaders working together in a way which would enable God's design to be produced.

In fact it has proved a key to understanding the whole life of the church as a complex, but potentially beautiful, pattern created by a series of almost unending interlocking circles of relationships through which individuals are sustained in their faith and sent out in service.

The church council: the initial leadership group

However one particular application was soon evident as far as the central management structures were concerned. As I thought about the spirograph picture, I saw how it helped to interpret our past. We had begun with a church council – the large solid circle (see previous page) – which had been *the* leadership group in the church.

As the years had passed a number of small groups had emerged out of this and begun to exercise significant leadership roles. First was the staff team. Then, particularly because of the great demands of the building project, the standing committee had taken on major administrative decision-making functions. More recently the wardens had been exercising a major role as trouble shooters and in their support and supervision of the staff team and its working.

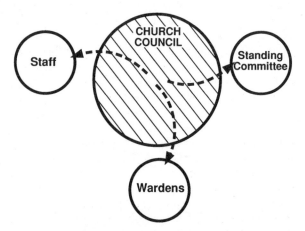

The phase of growth of small leadership groups

What now needed to happen then became clear. First the nature of the church council had changed and needed to be acknowledged. It had delegated many of its functions to these other groups. Its role was now like that of a boundary commission, defining the limits and monitoring the work of these groups and being a conduit for two-way communication between the leadership groups and the church. Second, those leadership groups needed consciously to come back within the ambit and authority of the council and be given authority to act on its behalf.

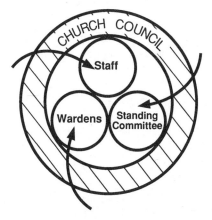

The emerging pattern

We are aware that this is dealing only with the *functional* aspect of this plateau. The *spiritual* level is in the process of being renewed through a fresh vision for the mission of each congregation. We have not yet fully released the *emotional* blockage to the burst of further growth which we look for.

Integrated Learning

I record this part of the story not primarily because of the organisational structure that emerged, but because of the interplay of the inspirational, intuitive and analytical elements in the resolution of our problems. In a striking way, the solution to our organisational confusion arose out of prayer and an exercise of the gifts of the Spirit. The super-spirituality triangle is back in place; we have been tasting a little of creation being renewed and redeemed.

No wonder we live in hope; because even as we live through this present development, preparing once more to move into the unknown, there is a sense of God continuing to teach the principles of leadership that we need to learn for the next stage of our pilgrimage as a community of believers.

Chapter Eleven

MANAGING TO SURVIVE

Two dramatic mistakes in my time in Wolverhampton helped me to recognise the pressures involved in the Christian ministry. Although they arose out of full-time work in the ordained ministry, the pressures of many forms of lay ministry have some of the same effects on those involved.

The first happened at the end of a long day on duty at the crematorium. During the afternoon I had taken five funerals, without a break, in two-and-a-half hours. After each service we always said: 'At this Sunday evening's service at the parish church we will be praying for the friends and relations of . . . and you are invited to join us.' They usually did, and so often there were more mourners than regular congregation at the service, as it was a large parish in which we regularly had fifteen funerals a week.

I had just shaken the hands of the last funeral group at the end of the final service, and was walking back to the vestry, when the undertaker caught up with me. 'You know what you said, do you, sir?' An instant action replay started in my mind and out of my subconscious I realised that instead of using the correct name of the deceased (which was Fanny Williams), I had said: 'This Sunday evening we will be praying for the friends and relations of Fanny Hill'! It was just after the celebrated 'obscene publications' trial. Horrified, I rushed back to the family and expressed my heartfelt apologies. They were very understanding and seemed to take it well, but for me it took several weeks to come to terms with that mistake.

Not that I had that long to recover before the next one. This time it was an afternoon baptism. It was due to take place at three o'clock and when I arrived at about quarter-to-three, I found the family sitting there. A strong sense of disapproval met me as I entered. They obviously considered me to be late for their big event. I threw on my robes as rapidly as I could and went straight ahead with the service; starting, I was convinced, several minutes early.

Five minutes into the service, I was just beginning to relax and unwind from the unnerving start when a terrible thought hit me like a thunderbolt. With my rushed entry, I had omitted my normal routine so that now I was high and dry – there was no water in the font! This time something within me determined I would not be beaten. I did not feel I had turned up late and I inwardly refused to make matters worse by apologising for not putting water in the font. There were just two prayers and the baptismal vows between me and disaster. I had to think fast. So, after the vows, I confidently announced, 'Will the congregation please be seated for the ceremony of the fetching of the water!' I proceeded to the font in as religious a manner as I knew how, picked up the bowl inside and slowly and solemnly processed to the kitchen of the dual purpose building. Once out of sight, I sped across the kitchen at top speed, filled the bowl, returned to the door and then with great dignity processed back again to the font, to continue the service. Everyone seemed most impressed and thanked me for the service.

Though amusing now, at the time these events were sharp reminders to me of the considerable pressure produced in a large parish where fifteen funerals a week and eight weddings on a Saturday were the norm. I felt as if I had fallen overboard into a fathomless sea of activity, demand and expectation which left me gasping for the fresh air of purpose in it all.

Life at St Thomas's has presented a very different set of pressures from those I experienced in Wolverhampton. The blessings of renewal brought enormous pressures as I was immersed in the hard school of conflict management. The joy of the building project was the fruit of five tough years of work, during which I felt as if the ministry was an additional job on top of my full-time work on the project. It left me physically, emotionally and spiritually drained in a way I did not realise at the time. The privilege of being in a growing church has involved the pain of a church coping with change which not infrequently has felt like bereavement. Losing our 'old' building, losing our straightforward Anglican identity, losing our way spiritually, losing the relative tranquillity of the days before the coming of the nine-o'clock service, have all been costly experiences. Losing my own role, only to find a new one emerging, has happened several times. I have been able to identify with the apostle Paul when he wrote: 'Besides everything else, I face daily the pressure of my concern for all the churches' (2 Cor 11.28).

Yet it was out of those moments of failure and embarrassment, such as I experienced at the funeral and baptism, and out of the continuing experience of pressure and stretching, that God has spoken to me. It has not been by some audible voice, or even 'word' which I could have written down, but rather through an awareness of an issue that has continually had to be faced. Anger at what seems to be overwhelming pressure has made me fight for direction and purpose. I have determined that I would find answers to the questions that surface through these experiences. Just what am I about? Where am I and the church heading – if anywhere? Where is his way? Behind all these questions was the nagging doubt as to whether I could 'manage' to survive.

Uncomfortable though the questions were, they were some of the most vital I have ever faced, particularly about how to handle the stress of Christian leadership on a long-term basis. I now realise the central importance of this to the whole of learning about leadership through experience. Unless we can handle the stresses which are unavoidably involved, we will never be able fully to exercise the insight we have acquired. Managing to survive is therefore not just about finding a way to survive somehow. It is about positively taking those steps which will enable us not only to survive, but actually to thrive on all that is required of us.

Before sharing the answers that have come, it is important to point out that the learning has, once again, been at the point of weakness. Indeed, incidents such as the ones I have related have built into me a deep confidence in God in those places. He seems to specialise in such opportunities for redemption. It is said that a drowning man can be a threat to his rescuer's life until he reaches the point of abandoning the fight: then is the time to step in to rescue him. I have known that pattern in my own life and God's ability to redeem (turn to good) any situation.

Making Costly Choices

Out of these experiences, and the pressures of so many expectations, came some intuitive responses and decisions. Faced with the reality of the spiritual battle, I soon saw that nerve would be needed to discover and work for God's purposes, rather than simply to flow with everyone's expectations of me.

First, there were hard decisions about other people's expectations of my role. Arriving in Wolverhampton, I was aware of the expectation that I would be a 'youth curate', because that was the main focus of the church. However, I made a deliberate choice, before God, to seek to build up the faith and life of the whole church, rather than just one aspect of its work. In the long run I gained the confidence of the church and proved the value of that decision, but in the short term it was not well received.

Coming to St Thomas's, I found the pressure of role expectation more subtle. The church had grown, and the desire was not to change a winning team. However, quite unconscious of the fact, the church was not wanting to grow: or rather, not wanting to pay the price of growth. There was considerable pressure for the vicar to know everyone pastorally; and that can happen only with a group of under two hundred. Yet the church was already up to that size. I had to decide either in effect to close the doors (and put a 'Church full' sign outside), or to find a different way of operating. That would involve a different relationship with the leader, and the trust of a new generation of lay leaders. It took time to achieve.

There was also the pressure from the local community and its expectation that the vicar would visit them. I was well aware that attempting to visit eight thousand people was a ridiculous task. Giving people half an hour each it would take two years if I spent sixty hours a week just on that. And what would be achieved? I saw that my task was to mobilise an army of people whose knowledge of God, and love for others, was such that they would be engaged in effective visiting of the whole community simply by being part of it.

Second, there were hard choices about having the courage to work for change. It is so easy to rest content with where we are, but I am sure it is more pleasing to God to hear the disturbing and creative notes of discontent. God is pleased when his people, and their leaders, dare to push on in seeking for more of him and a more evident display of his life in the church today. The urge to move forward, to grow, develop and change, is a precious leadership gift from God himself. If that is to happen we need to seek from God, not the ability to be encouraged with what is, but rather the courage to live and work for what is not yet: for the coming of the kingdom of God in ways we have still to experience. That sense of moving forward has to begin with the leader as a person, before it can touch the church.

Third, there was the need to move from a reactive to a pro-active style of ministry. It is so easy to allow the hopes and fears, as well as the demands and expectations, of others to dictate what we do. The leader, however, is called to lead, and that involves having the courage to say no. Growth would not happen by accident. I knew it would involve sustained hard work and the giving of strategic priority to purpose and direction. An unattributed quotation spoke to me about this:

> Quality is never an accident.
> It is always the result of intelligent effort.
> There must be the will to produce a superior thing.

The growth of the church is a gift of God and a work of his grace; but harvesting the fruit of that work of God is hard. Dogged endurance, not being willing to settle for less than the best, attention to detail, plenty of patience, sheer hard work, but above all the willingness to give priority to the things that matter most, have all been required. President Eisenhower said, 'The important things are rarely urgent, and the urgent things rarely important.' If I was to manage to survive, costly choices which cut across other people's expectations would be involved. But I soon came to realise that the benefit of those choices could outweigh the costs.

Following Jesus
As I wrestled with decisions about how to use my time, it was out

of the scriptures that God's inspiration and direction came to me. Luke's Gospel, chapter four, became a special chapter for me in learning how to survive in ministry. From his baptism, Jesus moves into a profound range of stresses and pressures and shows us how to handle them.

Jesus lived with a freedom which came from his obedience to the Father. I saw how demanding yet liberating that lifestyle was: continually seeking to discover what is pleasing to God, and yet able to say no where we do not sense the call of God on our lives. I saw how this sense of direction enabled Jesus to cope with the quite extra-ordinary pressures on him.

The chapter opens with Jesus responding to the call of the Father: 'Jesus, full of the Holy Spirit, returned from the Jordan and was led by the Spirit into the desert' (v1). God was setting his agenda. That was the first step I had to take, of making time to discover God's priorities and then to have the courage to put those things first. Immediately after this leading of the Spirit, however, Jesus experienced not elation but profound spiritual warfare in a place of total isolation. 'The devil said . . .' (v3). Vital choices which would affect the character he would become were made at that point. So with us, vital choices about our effectiveness are made in secret when we sense the pressure of ministry and how we will yield to, or confront, it. Life-changing decisions confront us in prayer as we listen to what is going on. Will we settle for putting our reputation first, for an easy life, or will we settle simply for the goal of keeping the organisation of the church going? These have been some of the 'voices in the wilderness' I have had to confront.

No sooner had Jesus dealt with those voices than he had to face the opposite situation; runaway success: 'All spoke well of him and were amazed at the gracious words that came from his lips' (v22). Success is as dangerous as outright attack, and Jesus holds fast to the Father's will and is not moved by such praise. How easy it is, at those moments of blessing and success which touch every ministry, to turn the glory from where it truly belongs, onto ourselves. Even more subtle and dangerous is to seek to live for those moments alone: to be addicted to success and achievement, and not able to go through the whole pattern of cross-and-resurrection as Jesus did. The person who desires to follow God's will for the church has to become able to handle success.

Immediately after coping with success, Jesus is faced with immense human hostility, 'All the people in the synagogue were furious . . . they got up, drove him out of town . . . in order to throw him down the cliff' (vv28,29). Though marginally less dangerous than success, because it more easily drives us to God and prayer, personal attack can knock us off balance. A letter sent to me during the building project was addressed to 'The Vandal of Crookes'. Others turned around on me the rich generosity of the church during that project and said, 'He's only interested in people's money.' Painful though those misrepresentations in the community are, it is the barbed comments of fellow believers which cut most deeply. 'Even my close friend whom I trusted, he who shared my bread, has lifted up his heel against me' (Ps 41.9).

The next step in his experience of ministry 'in the power of the Spirit' is to be confronted for the first time by a demon – 'What do you want with us, Jesus of Nazareth?' (v34) – just where all of us would least like to experience one: in a church service. Again Jesus holds on to the will of the Father and to his relationship which gives him the knowledge to deal with the problem.

Spiritual warfare on this level can be an immensely draining work. Those needing this help are often people with a number of problems, not least in establishing healthy relationships with others. My initial encounters in this area seemed to end up with long sessions late into the night. I now consider that enemy time, and have learned that it is I, under God, who have authority as to when and how such problems are dealt with. Taking authority is just what Jesus did.

Not surprisingly, the next experience of ministry which Jesus had was simply one of exhaustion. After dealing with the demonic interruption, he went on to heal Simon's mother-in-law. Then, with little or no time to recover, he spent the whole evening in such work. 'When the sun was setting, the people brought to Jesus all who had various kinds of diseases' (v40). Jesus deals with it not by going to bed, but by going to the Father. He, like us, needed to do both; but being at home with the Father was the secret both of his strength and of his rest. He had to fight for time for prayer and time for physical rest.

The final pressure comes from those who are enthusiastic for his healing ministry to continue. 'They tried to keep him from leaving them'(v42). That final test shows Jesus holding true to the call of God which he has taken time to discover; and so he goes off to preach to the other towns also. Undoubtedly those to whom it is most difficult to say no are those who are well known to us – including family and friends. Choosing the priorities that God gives will often make the leader feel like the odd one out, but our security can come only from pleasing God. I have already told something of the struggles I experienced both in Wolverhampton and Sheffield, to hold on to the life-line of God's agenda, rather than drown in a sea of endless expectations from others.

The example of Jesus has been a continual inspiration to me to seek to discover and do the will of God as best I know how, and as a consequence to dare to leave other things not done. It has also been the supreme model of how to manage to survive. Even for Jesus, doing the will of the Father was not one success after another, but rather a continual battle at the physical, emotional and spiritual levels to resist being diverted from the call of God. Yet, in the face of all those pressures and stresses, he modelled how to handle the strain. It is good to be able to bring to him all the reactions we experience in leading others, knowing that in this as much as anything else 'we do not have a high priest who is unable to sympathise with our weaknesses, but we have one who has been tempted in every way, just as we are – yet was without sin' (Heb 4.15).

Budgeting my Time

Making the right use of time was evidently a vital issue for Jesus in handling stress and he clearly made some major decisions about it. I came to realise that I also needed to make some important decisions about how to handle my own time.

Keeping a strategic eye on my particular role within the life of the church meant being wise about my use of time. There was so much developing in the life of the church that I could have worked every hour of every day and not done all that needed to be done. Nothing would be achieved by burn-out. I needed to work out a clear plan for the use of my time.

After many struggles I developed a simple analytical tool: a block-chart diary. Each morning, afternoon, or evening was a block of time. In each week I scheduled various blocks of work that needed to be included. So the staff fellowship over Monday lunch time and the staff meeting on Wednesday morning were blocked out. For desk work, correspondence and planning, I blocked out Monday and Thursday mornings.

The biggest struggle, and breakthrough, came over allocating time to think and pray and to prepare and plan ahead. For a long time I had told myself that when there was time I would go away to Whirlow Grange (the Sheffield diocesan conference centre, just twenty minutes drive away) and have a day quietly on my own. The problem was that there never was any spare time to do this. One week, so frustrated by the lack of preparation I had put into something, I resolved there and then to go away one day each week from then onwards. It took a few weeks because I had unavoidable commitments at that stage. Now, however, that has become a fixed part of my programme. Every Tuesday I am away at Whirlow, thinking, reading, praying and preparing, which is absolutely essential if I am to keep my eye on the Lord, and on his purposes for his church.

Other blocks are set aside for seeing people, whether in a counselling situation, or working with our team of six full-time staff on their particular responsibilities. One of the church-wardens pointed out that my programme left no time for a crisis. I now have that blocked out too. Not of course that I am sufficiently omniscient to know when or where a crisis will arise! However, this is the great advantage of budgeting time. My fear before was that it would make me and life very inflexible. In practice it has added order and flexibility together. If some crisis arises and fills up my desk work time, I can simply reallocate that work to the crisis block of time I had previously allocated.

The other step I took in drawing up my weekly diary was that I always omitted Friday, my day off. This meant that there was no space for me to take on engagements or be involved in activities on that day. It has been of tremendous importance for my own survival, sanity, and refreshment – as well as for the health of my

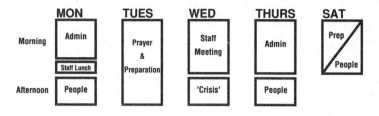

A typical weekly programme

marriage – to know that that time is never far away.

Handling time in this way has taken an important element of stress out of a demanding job. Before, whenever I was preparing a sermon I was worrying about when I could get letters written. Whenever I was doing those letters, I was concerned about when I would find time to see one of the staff team or lay leaders, and then when I did see that staff member I was wondering all the time if I should not be seeing Mrs So-and-so instead! Now, if while preparing a sermon, the thought of having a letter to write does cross my mind I know there is time allocated for that: and I know when that time is. That has taken much pressure out of my work.

Learning from Life

Three other steps have been a major help in learning to survive the experience of Christian leadership. They touch on the functional, emotional and spiritual levels of the problem I have been describing.

At the functional level I found it valuable to build back the rhythms of life into my lifestyle. We live in a very unnatural environment where many of the natural changes of pace have been removed from life. Jesus, pressurised though he was, frequently walked for three or more days on his journeys with his disciples. That inevitably enabled them to know each other well. It gave plenty of time for conversation, and plenty of time for quiet thinking. Today we go by fast means of transport across the city – or country, or world – from one meeting to another. Life in a twentieth-century urban environment seems to be all flow and no ebb.

Building back those rhythms has meant a number of simple practical steps.

First, making sure that I get a complete day off each week: and that it is the same day each week.

Second, discussing holidays with the church council (when I arrived in Crookes) so that I am taking what has been agreed with others (six weeks a year); this has removed any guilt about being away and makes for greater peace of mind.

Third, building in the regularity of a routine, such as always having Tuesday as my day for prayer and planning, and working set hours. Part of this involves an agreed time for the evening meal when we all sit down together to eat. We do not always make it, but overall there is a regularity and routine in both daily and weekly work. A change then feels just that – a departure from the norm. Having that routine eases the pressure considerably.

Fourth, developing routine 'habits of holiness' as I call them. For example, with an office at church five minutes walk from home, I have sought to use the walk always to pray (often in tongues). Once the routine became established I found I was doing it without thinking: which is the value of good routines.

At the emotional level I have found great value in learning to harness anger rather than suppress it. I now see anger as energy for life if it is well used. So, if something goes wrong, or I feel put on by others, or some other pressure begins to tell, I resist the temptation to be 'noble' and suppress my feelings. Rather I seek to look at them, own them, and harness them to dealing with the problem. Anger can be very creative. Indeed, anger is emotional fire. In its raw and uncontrolled state it can do enormous harm. When harnessed, it is one of the most powerful, creative and essential forces known to man. We depend on fire for the warmth of our homes, for virtually all means of transport, and for light. Anger too, can generate compassion, provide us with the motive power for change, and throw great light on the path ahead. Thus it gives the motivation to confront a problem that has been accepted until now. The result can be a permanent improvement: as long, of course, as Paul's words are heeded – 'Be angry but do not sin' (Eph 4.26). Anger must be used creatively rather than destructively.

At the spiritual level I have discovered the vital importance of meditation in times of testing and stress. Recently, in such a time I felt just like Martha, troubled by many things. As I deliberately sat down in a comfortable chair and stilled myself before God I heard him say, 'Be held together by the One, not distracted by the many.' What had happened was that I had lost my centering upon God and was being pulled apart by many conflicting demands. I needed to come back to him and to still myself in his presence. This, incidentally, is evidence, if the reader needs it, that what I have already written is not in the past tense with everything in my life now calm and ordered. Rather, I write in the present continuous tense with many lessons having to be learned over and over again – at a deeper level each time.

The practice of meditation is a wonderful life-line to God. It has also become inextricably bound up with a very practical action which has also been of enormous help in enabling me to survive under pressure – namely, list making. I do this in two ways. Especially when I am about to go home, I take just three minutes to be still and make a list of all the things I feel are needing attention. I allow my anxieties to surface in this way, and make a note of them. I can then assure them that they are not forgotten. However, I leave the list on my desk, which signals to me that the problems have been left at work, and are to remain there until I return. In this way I use stillness to uncover tasks that await to be done, and clear out the anxious clutter within.

List making also comes to my aid when I want my attention to be on God – especially when I spend time in prayer at the beginning of the day. The words of C. S. Lewis, in *Mere Christianity*, exactly describe my frequent experience:

> That is why the real problem of the Christian life comes where people do not usually look for it. It comes the very moment you wake up each morning. All your wishes and hopes for the day rush at you like wild animals. And the first job each morning consists simply in shoving them all back; in listening to that other voice, taking that other point of view, letting that other larger, stronger, quieter life come flowing in.

Making lists is my way of shoving back all those wild animals; again telling them that they have not been forgotten, but that I will not worship them and give them attention due only to God. They must wait their turn.

The Learning Cycle

The on-going reality of learning leadership from experience, particularly in relation to dealing with the pressures, was brought home vividly to me during the period of writing this book. On two occasions I experienced as deep a sense of despair and depression as I have ever felt. It was associated with a number of issues. I had simply become over-committed both inside and outside the church and was overwhelmed by the work I had to do. Then I was aware that, because I am more naturally an intuitive leader, it was difficult for others to fit in with my way of working – which is sometimes as unpredictable as it is creative. We were also going through major but subtle changes that I have earlier described as arising from our moving to a 'large church mode'. Yet I was still the person looked to for a host of detailed decisions as well as for leadership in strategy and development. Having learned to be pro-active, and see the church grow as a result, I was slow to see that that very growth was causing me to respond reactively – though this time in an even bigger way with a larger size of operation.

Having built in supports to my ministry, I was able to share exactly how I felt – describing the emotions rather than just identifying the problems – both with the wardens and with the staff team. They reacted creatively and lovingly, telling me not to do some things, and actually taking some tasks from me. It was a great help to be told what to do rather than just to be offered help if I needed it. They also gave support and help with the things I could not avoid. Furthermore, they applied their minds to the underlying problems and came up with solutions to them. Above all, lovingly, they helped me to see where I was my own worst enemy and where I needed to change. Confrontation was part of their love. They dealt with the functional, emotional, and spiritual dimensions to the problem.

The result has been a radical change in the staff team roles, including my withdrawal from the day-to-day decision making of the church, in order to be released to put strategic thinking, resources and input back into the church. My role has been defined in terms of developing the overall strategy and vision and the leadership of the staff team. Many other responsibilities have had to be shed.

It is a process which is far from complete but which I share in order to illustrate the fact that lessons we learn often have to be learned again and again as the circumstances change. Nowadays, five funerals in an afternoon or bone-dry fonts are not something I have to contend with. Managing to survive is nonetheless something I have always, and presumably will always, have to contend with. My conviction is that if God is committed to bringing about growth through our leadership, he is even more committed to bringing about growth in us to handle its consequences. It is an important part of the anvil of experience with which he lovingly, yet strongly, chooses to shape us according to his will. The extent to which this happens in practice depends on our willingness to engage, on his terms, with the process of learning which he continually offers.

Chapter Twelve

KEEPING GOING

The young lady hardly fitted the somewhat down-at-the-heels bunch of people at our small mid-week communion. She was young, attractive and very smartly dressed. She was up from London and had been brought to the service by a friend. It so happened that the Bible reading included Paul's advice to Timothy to 'flee youthful passions'. It was our custom to have silence after the reading and then to invite comments. After a short pause the young lady said in a strong and confident voice, 'What's wrong with a bit of passion?'

The answer, which did not come immediately to my lips, must be, 'It all depends what sort.' I want to end on a note of appropriate passion, by expressing just how crucial the art of learning leadership from experience has been to me even during the year in which this book has been in the writing. Moreover, I want to urge you, the reader, into this way of working with God, or if you are already on the road, to encourage you to keep going on that journey of discovery. The glorious prize is nothing less than God's truth so grasping us as people that it becomes written into our very personalities. God's desire, with which we set out at the beginning of this book, is that the truth be incarnate in us.

Still on the Anvil
Somewhere deep down I think I must have had the notion that once I had learned the ropes of being a vicar (perhaps after two or three years), I could settle into the job and take it in my stride.

Here I am now, eighteen years later, feeling as much a learner as ever I have done.

Though outwardly it might have looked a 'successful' year with the publication of my first book, *In the Crucible*, the truth is that it has been one of the most testing years so far. Twice before in my time at St Thomas's I have found myself making a major job change. Both of them were gradual evolutionary changes which I only grasped intuitively some time after the process had begun.

When I arrived at St Thomas's I was functioning in a fairly traditional (no criticism intended) *pastoral* role, getting to know, and to nurture in Christ, the two hundred or so people who formed the church at that time.

Somewhere along the line – towards the end of the seventies – I moved into what I can only describe as an *entrepreneurial* phase, in which my main role in the church was seeing through a series of major developments, beginning with the building project. The local ecumenical project followed, and then the nine o'clock service and the establishing of congregations. However, over the past year I have begun to see that a new phase has begun, involving further testing transition. This has involved me in coming to terms with being primarily *chairman* of a team of people who are working both as pastors and as leaders of developments within the church. This does not mean that I no longer care for people, or have ceased to be involved in major developments. It has, however, involved me in a major shift of roles.

Such shifts are never accomplished without significant personal changes and cost; it is always a stretching experience. The framework for learning has, however, been an invaluable guide in yet more uncharted waters.

I had learned, in previous testing times on the anvil of experience, to own my feelings and not hide them from myself or others. So I was quicker than before to allow my *intuition* to admit to the strain I felt under, which was precipitating the need to change roles once more. I have already told of the occasions of depression and of the ready support I received from others. This was the crucial first step without which there could have been no solution to my problems because there would have been no admission that there was a problem.

I was glad to see that my confidence in God having answers was such that I was eager to face the problems squarely. Those problems had to do with the sheer work load I was carrying and with the fact that everything seemed to hinge on me. Despite massive levels of delegation, whenever anyone wanted a quick and authoritative answer the standard means was to 'ask Robert'. I knew that this was no way for me to survive, let alone for the church to function in a healthy way.

The next step was to *analyse* what was going on. The process by which we received a picture from God about circles of teams of leaders, through the image of a spirograph design, has already been described. We were in the process of re-ordering the structures of the church so that it did not all depend on me in the way it had done in the past.

While that analysis of the church's structures was going on, a more personal analysis was carried out as well. With the encouragement of the staff and wardens, for a whole month I made a log of everything I did in my work, broken down into units of a quarter of an hour. It was a hard but revealing exercise. Others then did the detailed analysis needed to identify what I simply had to stop doing and what my new priorities should be.

Alongside this, God's *inspiration* came in several ways. The word about 'being held together by the One, not distracted by the many' was part of the way that God spoke. A very simple dream woke me up one night with a start. In the dream I 'saw' my car parked with the wheels on full lock. I was standing beside it and realised – with horror – that all the tyres were completely bald. I woke up in a sweat of anxiety, yet convinced that I had in fact had them changed recently, and that I need not worry. When I became fully awake, I recalled that I had indeed changed all four tyres less than a year before. I felt relieved, but puzzled. Why had I had the dream? Then I saw that the Lord was speaking to me about my journey through life. I had been driving hard, not taking the time to service my own heart. I was reminded of the striking words of Martin Luther, who said 'I am now so busy that I cannot get through my work with less than three hours prayer a day.' If I did not give priority to time with him, I would have no protection in a crisis. In a number of other ways his word came to me calling me to be still before him, and to allow all ministry to grow out of that intimacy – rather than for the relationship to be crowded out by the ministry I was involved in.

Learning about Learning
Two striking insights came to me during this period. The first was that the pattern of learning I had been through was the same as the one I had previously identified as the pattern of the church's growth. God's desire for my growth as a person, and his plans for the growth (in quality as well as quantity) of the church I lead, are inextricably interwoven.

The graph I used in an earlier chapter to illustrate the pattern of repeated church growth, followed first by plateau, next by breakthrough, and then by a further growth phase, was also a mirror image of my own growth. Breaking through the church plateau has always first involved some new point of personal growth for me. It has been a humbling, yet deeply motivating experience to recognise that when I responded to the call of God in some area of personal growth, a further phase of development seemed to have been released for the church.

Through this insight I have heard the call of God never to settle down, nor even to be happy to settle for less than his best for myself or the church. God has good purposes of further fruitfulness

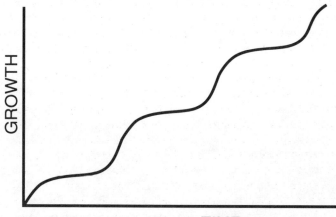

TIME

Personal growth parallels church growth

in store for the church. I do not want them to be missed because of failure, or unwillingness, on my part to go through what is involved in a new experience of God-inspired breakthrough.

The second insight about the nature of the learning process is that the framework for learning I have developed is not a fixed mechanical model, but a living and growing reality. Every testing time expands the frontiers of my experience at all three points of intuition, analysis and inspiration. This is why God is so eager to take me continually onto the anvil. He intends, out of his love for me and the church I serve, to expand the horizons of my knowledge of his ways in the sense of truly knowing him, rather than just having information about him.

Increasingly I see a new dimension to his call to me along the pilgrim way. Each testing step increases my grasp of his grace and nature. Yet that development of my personal intimacy with him is dynamically interwoven with his development of my ability to lead the church to which he has, for the present, called me.

Such are the reasons for the passion I feel for being open to learning in testing places. It is because, after all the transitions in leadership that God has enabled me to make so far, I am still experiencing the heat of the anvil. I am continually being made to recognise that – painful and stretching though it is – it is the place

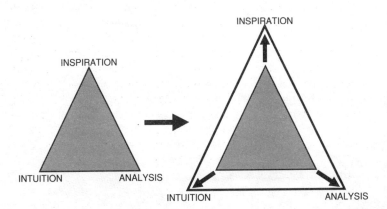

New dimensions in the learning experience

to which God calls all leaders, because it is the only place where leadership that pleases God can grow.

Arrival Syndrome
Yet I still have to be honest and admit that something else holds me back, and I know I am not alone in such an experience. Many of us feel there must be a by-pass to having to go this way, or maybe we feel we have actually arrived and our travelling days are done. Certainly few of us would say that we had 'made it' or 'arrived', but therein lies the danger. We might never say we have arrived, masking the fact that that may actually be our underlying philosophy. We need to face the possibility that our actions betray that we are caught in what I call the 'arrival syndrome'.

As the leader now of a so-called larger church, I am aware that such churches are particularly susceptible to catching this disease. It is contracted when a church which is growing does so because it is finding answers to the problems that inhibit growth. When this happens others hear of its success and start asking it questions about how their own problems can be solved. Before long so many questions are being asked that the trap is sprung: the larger church believes it has all the answers. It then becomes an ecclesiastical answering machine, which stops asking questions, and learning from others, but which instead gears itself up to tell everyone else the answers. The prognosis for such a church is that its heyday will soon end, for the hand of death is upon it. One of the clearest evidences of this is that leaders of such churches can usually only be found on the platforms of conferences – giving answers. All too rarely does one meet them on the conference floor, asking new questions, and hungry to learn.

What is true for churches about the arrival syndrome is equally true for us as individuals, especially leaders. Two particular hindrances can impede our continuing on the pilgrim path of learning from experience. One has to do with uncertainty about which way we should be seeking to go, the other has to do with lethargy about moving anywhere.

Confusing Signposts
Uncertainty about the direction God has for us or for the church

is often the first hindrance we encounter on our path to further learning and growth. Signposts certainly exist but their contradictory nature can inhibit any movement, and obscure our understanding of what God actually wants for his church.

One of the signposts which can cause much confusion is the *prosperity gospel*. This is a subtle distortion of God's generous promises to protect and provide. His promises are re-shaped to imply that if you simply believe enough, pray enough, or do the following eight things, then all will go well with you economically, socially and spiritually. When this attitude is propagated in a culture which is focused on material security, then distortion of the gospel takes place, and confusion of direction results. The goal of obedience to the Father's will is no longer the loving response of the redeemed. What results instead is an expression of modern man's desire to control his world – including even God. The motivation for Christian action is changed from a response of love to calculating self-advantage. No wonder we should want to run a mile from that direction for us as leaders, or for the church or group we lead.

The trouble is that we easily run too far along an equally dangerous track in the opposite direction, and end up in a *poverty mentality*. This approach to life, and especially church life, glories in failure. It is how much of Western (particularly European) Christianity has handled the dramatic decline in its membership and influence in the twentieth century. Rather than facing the harsh reality of our plight and coming before God in order to find the answers to our lack of fruitfulness for him, and to the underlying failure of nerve which is one of our chief characteristics, the Western church has developed a marvellous insulation against reality. Jesus, so the argument runs, seemed to the world to have failed, to be 'despised and rejected'. So, the reasoning continues, the church which obeys him must always expect to be a despised minority. Any sign of 'success' would be evidence of unfaithfulness to the gospel. With such a theology to explain our failure, we can rest content and let the world ignore and misunderstand us. It has a fatalism even greater than the most rigid forms of Calvinism.

Neither of these opposite paths leads us into God's direction for us. The teaching of the Bible, which can be described as the story of God in mission, is that his church should be fruitful: indeed successful. However, the definition of the success which is pleasing to God is that given in scripture – which integrates suffering and success, pain and fruitfulness.

It was painful to be Joseph – 'You intended to harm me, but God intended it for good to accomplish what is now being done, the saving of many lives' (Gen 50.20) – but God prospered his work. For Abraham, the 'success' of being the father of many nations grew out of being willing to sacrifice 'your son, your only son, whom you love' (Gen 22). For Joshua the promise of God was without qualification since he was told that God's commands were given 'that you may be successful wherever you go' (Jos 1.7). Yet entry into the promised land was a hard experience involving costly struggle. Indeed, warfare rather than success was to be the dominant note.

The key to their experience, and indeed to that which God wants for us as leaders and for his church, is that we are successful, but it is *a success measured by the cross and the resurrection*. It enters into and feels all the pain, hurt, sin, failure, and naked spiritual hostility that are part of human reality, and in the midst of, and out of the experience of that weakness, discovers the reality of the grace of God. That is success built on our humility by the overflowing grace of God. One of the chief marks of such success ('fruitfulness' is a more biblical term) built on this cross-and-resurrection pattern is that it does not threaten. It is 'touched with the feeling of our infirmities'. It is not about what man has achieved, but about what he has received. It is typical of such success that Paul, in writing about giving, points not to the materially richest church (maybe the church of Laodicea, in Revelation 3, qualifies for that doubtful distinction), but rather to the people of poverty.

> We want you to know about the grace that God has given the Macedonian churches. Out of the most severe trial, their overflowing joy and their extreme poverty welled up in rich generosity.
>
> (2 Cor 8.1–2)

The church contributed poverty, and availability – they were as malleable metal on the anvil of adversity – but God gave the gift of giving. That is a marvellous picture of holy success. It expresses the very antithesis of the arrival syndrome, namely the success of God's grace in the context of human poverty. That is truth incarnate in the people of God – his ultimate goal.

Down with Encouragement

The path to such holy success can often be imperilled by a second, and surprising, hindrance – namely, encouragement. This is one of the most overworked words in the Christian vocabulary today. It is also one of the most dangerous and debilitating; but we hear it on every side. Ask any church member how things are going in their church and, almost always, you will find that, 'We are very encouraged.' Ask the same question of ministers and you will find this to be even more consistently the case.

A question, and an answer, alerted me to some danger signs about all this encouragement. The question which puzzled me was *why is everyone always encouraged*, when we live in a century that has seen the most sustained period of decline of church membership in this country since the gospel first came to our shores?

It is a normal form of conversation between ministers to greet one another by saying. 'How are things going in your church?' One recent answer to me was: 'We are really quite encouraged: our numbers at the morning services have been falling at a slower rate than they were last year!' I realised what potential there is for encouragement in this approach. Practically every church can be 'encouraged' that no one has embezzled the funds all week! In other words, if you set the target low enough everyone is a winner. But what sort of victory is that?

A simple group-work exercise on team leadership I was involved in recently drew my attention to further evidence of the dangers of this attitude. The group had ten minutes to build as tall a tower as they could with the newsprint, string, tape and scissors provided. One group had some brilliant ideas, but worked as six individuals, and failed completely. In the discussion afterwards, everyone was trying to encourage everyone else. 'It was a great idea', 'we nearly made it', 'if it had not been for the length of the piece of string', 'we did not have enough time' and so on. In response to total disaster the group united around a 'ministry of encouragement'. The message was so clear – 'it's O.K. to fail'. But is it?

Encouragement is a fine Christian ministry. Barnabas ('son of encouragement') is one of the most attractive characters in the New Testament. He practised a ministry of encouragement to others wherever he saw the grace of God at work. But there is no evidence that he refused to face facts and admit failure when that was needed.

However, the modern church's understanding of encouragement is built on poor foundations. Such encouragement seems so Christian, yet if it causes us to avoid the truth of our situation, and to protect us from reality, it is obviously hindering the purposes of God. It is another form of the arrival syndrome which it is all too easy to fall into and from which we need to find God's help to break free.

Up with Courage

What then is the antidote to such false 'encouragement', and what is the God-honouring motivation needed to keep us learning and growing as leaders? It is *courage*. Four aspects of the exercise of that courage have stood out for me as I have sought to maintain my commitment to journeying forward in learning leadership.

First is the courage to take risks. As someone has said, 'The man who never made a mistake never made anything.' Not that I want to counsel foolish risk-taking for the sake of the risk. But the taking of risk is a sign of life. It is evidence of the attempt to take a step forward, of keeping moving.

Certainly for us at St Thomas's, risk-taking has been a part of every move forward. Opening up to the charismatic dimension was a risk: so was launching into the massive building project: as were the decisions to unite with the Baptist church, and develop an urban youth culture congregation. Faith is not certainty, but the confidence to face the uncertainty of risk-taking. A small and declining church has little to risk as it seeks to change and adapt. The more it grows the more is at stake in risk-taking. Unless the leadership can remain open, the point is reached when too much is at stake to take any more risks. Unless that is faced the consequent outbreak of the arrival syndrome will prove fatal.

Second is the courage to face failure. The 'encouragement' mentality looks like faith – being positive, putting a brave face on things, hoping for the best, looking for the good in a situation. Yet actually it is based on fear: fear of facing the facts. Such fear of acknowledging failure where it exists is the fruit of unbelief. God's grace is sufficient for all our needs; but it cannot get through if we insist on denying that need. It is this denial which allows unbelief to become established. The moment of break-through for the prodigal son happened when 'he came to his senses', and admitted the mess he was in. Faith, if it is ever to work in leadership, requires the courage to face failure, not to pretend it does not exist.

Third is the courage to be creatively discontent. This is crucial if we are to avoid settling down, and thinking we have arrived. Like Abraham we have to act on the truth that 'here we have no continuing city' (Heb 13.14). There are two worlds with which the church is engaged. One is the reality of the situation we are in, the other is (or should be) our vision of the situation that God is wanting to create. This 'vision' is expressed by Jesus in terms of the 'now' and the 'not yet', of the kingdom of God. Living with this double focus presents the Christian with a basic decision of whether to treat reality or vision as the fixed point.

The situation is like one of those physics experiments many of us can remember from school when a spark was made to jump between two metal points by passing an electrical current of sufficient strength between the two. All I can remember is the principle of 'the bigger the gap, the bigger the spark, and the bigger the current that is needed'. So it is with the Spirit. The bigger the gap between the reality of the situation we are in, and the vision we have of what God wants to do among us, the greater is our need to see even more of God's power flowing. Greater also is the place that prayer and faith will have to play if we are to see the vision becoming reality.

A perpetual state of false 'encouragement' simply closes the gap, and minimises the expectancy about the spark of God's action. What is needed in such a situation is the creative gift of discontent! However apparently unwelcome, *dis*couragement and *dis*satisfaction are prerequisites for movement to be instigated. Courage has to be exercised for these to find appropriate creative means of expression.

Fourth is the courage to pray the prayer of despair, however strange that may sound. 'I have heard of the prayer of faith,' I can almost hear the reader say, 'but the prayer of despair, what is that?'

Despair is in fact foundational to much biblical prayer. Joseph in prison, far from home, with no hope of justice is in despair – and turns to God in prayer. Nehemiah, distressed about the state of Jerusalem, knows that, as cup bearer to the king, he has no way in which he can do anything about it – and in that attitude of total dependence, prays to God. Hannah, childless, cries out in such despair that Eli mistakes her for a drunk. Hezekiah, told by Isaiah that he is about to die, cries out in despair. Blind Bartimaeus, ignoring all calls to behave himself and not embarrass people around him, cries out in despair to Jesus. And Jesus, in despair, turns to the Father in his cry, 'My God, my God, why have you forsaken me?' How unlike our emotionless, casual, vague, and take-it-or-leave-it praying are these desperate prayers which are so full of passion.

Biblical prayer, I have concluded, is founded on a clear awareness of the helplessness and hopelessness of our situation. That is the powerful energising force of its prayer life. The prayer of despair is the path to hope.

Of course, despair which actually despairs of God is unbelief. What I am talking about is despair that turns to God. Read the Psalms and you will see how full of complaints they are. The faith of the psalmist is evidenced by the fact that the complaints are addressed to God. At the deepest point faith is the courage to despair *to* God.

Heroes of the Faith
The call of God to Christian leaders today is to keep going on in our availability to him so that his church may bear fruit. For that to happen we must avoid the twin dangers of a false triumphalism (the prosperity gospel), or a distorted humility (the poverty mentality), and strike out in courageous faith to follow him. This should not be just for the church or group we lead, but for us as

individuals; because it is through our growth that much of his purposes for his church will be fulfilled.

On this pilgrim way we have the profound privilege to be part of the 'communion of saints' which transcends time, and which through the ages has drawn inspiration from the courage of the heroes of faith, so graphically described in Hebrews chapter eleven. Abraham, our father in the faith, is presented as the greatest model for us:

> By faith Abraham, when called to go to a place he would later receive as his inheritance, obeyed and went, even though he did not know where he was going.
>
> (Heb. 11.8)

But Abraham is not the only witness to the joy of keeping going in the purposes of God along the pilgrim way, to whom the scriptures point. We are indeed surrounded by a great cloud of witnesses to the faithfulness of God towards those who exercise the courage to keep going to their dying day.

Keeping Going

Jesus knew just how powerful pictures are in communicating truth. Two such visual aids to faith have impressed themselves upon me as I have sought to discover from God how to communicate the passion which Paul felt for keeping going in personal growth as a leader. These pictures have come to me in prayer and have helped me to see afresh the urgency of God's call to keep going.

The first picture is of the annual cycle in a wheat field. Every year it is ploughed up, then sown with seed which is nurtured until harvest, when the crop is taken, and then the whole annual process begins again with a further ploughing up of the soil. It is like that in following God. At the moment of greatest fruitfulness and maturity the divine harvester comes along to turn all the soil over and to begin afresh. Unless there is a continual inner conversion and growth there can be no continuous harvest: only a once-off blessing. I now know that the sense of arrival and of having conquered some major phase or task is the point at which to look for a new beginning. Leadership which desires to sustain renewal has to learn to welcome the return of the plough. C. S.

Lewis expresses this call of God to a deeply worked conversion when, in *Mere Christianity*, he writes:

> The terrible thing, the almost impossible thing, is to hand over your whole self – all your wishes and precautions – to Christ. But it is far easier than what we are all trying to do instead. For what we are trying to do is to remain what we call 'ourselves', to keep personal happiness as our great aim in life, and yet at the same time be 'good' . . . And this is exactly what Christ warned us you could not do. As He said, a thistle cannot produce figs. If I am a field that contains nothing but grass-seed, I cannot produce wheat. Cutting the grass may keep it short: but I shall still produce grass and no wheat. If I want to produce wheat, the change must go deeper than the surface. I must be ploughed up and re-sown.

The second picture is of the ancient milestones along a road. They are full of character and interest, and it is tempting to set up camp beside them; but that is to miss the whole point of their being there. They are there to encourage us along the way towards our destination. They were never intended to be stopping places. How tragic it is to see individual leaders, and whole groups of believers, setting up camp around some past event of great significance and missing the point that such happenings are only milestones, not the destination itself. We are on an urban clearway. Here we have no continuing city.

Readiness to keep learning on the anvil of experience is the only way that leadership can continue to grow and bear fruit, the rich harvest of God's truth burnt into our souls and made incarnate in us. The calling of God to the Christian leader is to respond to his grace by exercising the courage to go the full distance.

by the same author

IN THE CRUCIBLE

'An impressive and helpful work that ought to be read by all interested in evangelism.'

Church Times

'Brilliant.'

Canon Michael Green

'A clear perspective on both their exciting growth and their times of testing, over 18 years.'

Church of England Newspaper

'Dramatic.'

The Christian Herald

'An inspiring read, not just for your vicar . . .'

21 CC

'Absolutely magnificent.'

Canon Michael Harper

'One of those rare Christian books one would have liked to have gone on longer.'

In Gear, United Reformed Church